PEACEFUL EASY TRAVEL

Exploring Santa Barbara County

Insider Insights from a Local Resident for Your Ultimate Travel Experience

Copyright © 2024 by Brandee Jankoski

All rights reserved. No part of this publication may be reproduced, stored or transmitted in any form or by any means, electronic, mechanical, photocopying, recording, scanning, or otherwise without written permission from the publisher. It is illegal to copy this book, post it to a website, or distribute it by any other means without permission.

First edition

*This book was professionally typeset on Reedsy.
Find out more at reedsy.com*

Contents

1	Introduction	1
	Welcome to Santa Barbara County: An Overview	1
	What Makes Santa Barbara Unique: Geography, Climate, and Culture	2
	How to Use This Guide: Tips for Planning Your Trip	2
2	Getting to Know Santa Barbara County	4
	Brief History of the Area	4
	Overview of the County's Geography: Major Towns and Natural Landmarks	6
	The Climate and Best Times to Visit	8
3	Santa Barbara: The Heart of The County	11
	Downtown Santa Barbara: Must-Visit Spots and Historical Landmarks	11
	The Santa Barbara Mission: A Dive into Its History and Present-Day Significance	14
	Beaches and Parks: A Guide to Enjoying Santa Barbara's Natural Beauty	16
	Dining Choices in Santa Barbara	18
4	Beyond Santa Barbara – Exploring the County	41
	The Santa Ynez Valley: Wineries, Horseback Riding, and Danish Charm in Solvang	41
	Carpinteria: Beaches, Avocados, and Family-Friendly Activities	54
	Montecito: Luxury, Gardens, and Celebrity Sightings with Exquisite Dining	56
5	Activities and Experiences	69

	Outdoor Adventures in Santa Barbara: Hiking, Surfing, and Kayaking	69
	Cultural Experiences in Santa Barbara: Museums, Galleries, and Theaters	72
	Family Fun in Santa Barbara	78
6	Events and Festivals	82
	Annual Highlights in Santa Barbara: Seasonal Events and Festivals	82
	July to September: Summer Fun and Cultural Celebrations	94
	October to December: Harvest and Holidays	102
7	Planning Your Trip	110
	Accommodations in Santa Barbara: From Luxury Resorts to Cozy Bed and Breakfasts	110
	Transportation in Santa Barbara County: Navigating by Car, Public Transport, and Bike	113
8	Itineraries	115
	Itinerary 1: The Weekend Getaway – A 2-Day Trip Focusing on the Highlights	115
	Itinerary 2: Family Vacation – A 5-Day Plan with Family-Friendly Activities	117
	Itinerary 3: The Outdoor Enthusiast – A Week-Long Adventure Exploring Nature	119
9	Local Tips and Tricks	123
	Insider Knowledge: How to Avoid the Crowds and Make the Most of Your Visit	123
10	Conclusion	126
	Parting Words: Encouragement to Explore and Create Your Own Santa Barbara Story	126
	Resources: Further Reading and Useful Websites for Planning Your Trip to Santa Barbara	128
11	Appendices	131
	Accommodations Contact Information:	131
	Adventures	132

Links to Maps of Santa Barbara

1

Introduction

Welcome to the enchanting world of Santa Barbara County, a gem on California's Central Coast that promises an unforgettable journey through its stunning landscapes, rich cultural tapestry, and vibrant communities. As a local who grew up in the heart of this beautiful county, specifically in Goleta, I'm thrilled to share the insider knowledge and deep love I hold for my hometown and its surroundings. Santa Barbara County, with its unique blend of natural beauty, diverse climates, and a rich blend of cultures, has always been a place close to my heart. It's where I learned to appreciate the delicate balance between preserving natural beauty and embracing cultural evolution.

Welcome to Santa Barbara County: An Overview

Nestled between the rugged Santa Ynez Mountains and the Pacific Ocean, Santa Barbara County spans a diverse geographical area that includes everything from serene beaches to lush vineyards and rolling hills. The county is home to several charming towns and cities, each with its own unique character and attractions. From the bustling streets of downtown Santa Barbara to the Danish-inspired town of Solvang and the serene beauty of Carpinteria, this guide will take you through the heart and soul of the region, uncovering its many treasures.

What Makes Santa Barbara Unique: Geography, Climate, and Culture

Geography: Santa Barbara's geography is as varied as it is stunning. With over 100 miles of coastline, mountain ranges, and valleys, the region offers many natural beauty. The Channel Islands National Park, a short boat trip away, is a pristine natural sanctuary providing nature lovers a unique adventure.

Climate: The area enjoys a year-round Mediterranean climate characterized by mild, wet winters and dry, warm summers. This perfect weather allows for various outdoor activities in all seasons, from surfing and kayaking in the Pacific to hiking in the Los Padres National Forest.

Culture: Santa Barbara's culture combines Spanish colonial heritage, bohemian arts, and a laid-back California lifestyle. The county is renowned for its culinary scene, which includes farm-to-table restaurants, world-class wineries, and vibrant farmers' markets. Its cultural calendar is packed with festivals, art shows, and live performances, reflecting its communities' diverse and dynamic spirit.

How to Use This Guide: Tips for Planning Your Trip

This travel guide is your companion to discovering the best of Santa Barbara County. It's structured to give you an in-depth look at each area's attractions, activities, and hidden gems. Here are a few tips to help you make the most of

INTRODUCTION

this guide:

- **Prioritize Your Interests:** Whether interested in outdoor adventures, cultural experiences, or relaxation, focus on the chapters and sections that resonate with your travel goals.
- **Use the Itineraries:** Check out the suggested itineraries to help plan your visit, whether you're staying for a weekend or longer.
- **Local Tips and Tricks:** The insider advice scattered throughout the guide can help you experience Santa Barbara like a local, from avoiding tourist traps to discovering off-the-beaten-path spots.
- **Plan According to Season:** While Santa Barbara's climate is welcoming year-round, some activities and events are seasonal. Use this guide to align your travel dates with the experiences that interest you most.

Armed with this guide, you're well on your way to experiencing the enchanting beauty, rich culture, and unforgettable adventures Santa Barbara County offers. Let's embark on this journey together, uncovering the magic of the American Riviera, one page at a time.

2

Getting to Know Santa Barbara County

Brief History of the Area

Santa Barbara County's history is a vibrant mosaic that reflects the changing faces of the civilizations that have called it home. This area has witnessed the ebb and flow of human activity, each layer adding depth and color to its story.

The Chumash Era: Long before European explorers set foot on these shores, the Chumash people thrived across what is now Santa Barbara County. Renowned for their sophisticated maritime skills, the Chumash navigated the waters in plank canoes known as tomols, reaching as far as the Channel Islands. Their communities were rich in culture and artistry, evident from the intricate basketry, rock art, and beadwork that have been preserved. The Chumash also developed a complex social system and made significant astronomical and environmental observations, which guided their farming and fishing practices.

Spanish Exploration and Mission Period: The arrival of Spanish explorer Juan Rodríguez Cabrillo in 1542 marked the beginning of European interest in the region, but it wasn't until the establishment of the Mission Santa

Barbara in 1786 that significant European settlement began. This period saw the Spaniards introducing new agriculture, livestock, and architectural styles, notably the mission buildings that still stand today. However, this era also brought diseases and a new social order that profoundly impacted the indigenous populations.

Mexican Independence: After Mexico gained independence from Spain in 1821, Santa Barbara County became part of the Mexican Republic. During this time, large tracts of land were granted to individuals, leading to the rise of the ranchero culture. This era is characterized by the expansion of cattle ranching and a blending of Mexican and indigenous cultures, which significantly shaped the region's social and economic landscape.

American Incorporation and Growth: The conclusion of the Mexican-American War in 1848 and the subsequent incorporation of California into the United States ushered in a new phase of development. The discovery of oil in the late 19th and early 20th centuries transformed the economy of Santa Barbara County, attracting investment and workers. The region also became a haven for artists, writers, and filmmakers, drawn by its scenic beauty and mild climate.

Modern Developments: In the 20th century, Santa Barbara County emerged as a premier destination for tourism, agriculture, and education, with the establishment of institutions like the University of California, Santa Barbara. The area has also faced challenges, including environmental disasters like oil spills and wildfires, which have shaped local conservation efforts and community resilience.

Preservation and Future: Today, Santa Barbara County balances its rich historical heritage with the demands of modern development. Efforts to preserve the natural environment, historical sites, and cultural heritage are evident across the county, reflecting a commitment to honoring the past while embracing a sustainable future.

Overview of the County's Geography: Major Towns and Natural Landmarks

Santa Barbara County, nestled along California's breathtaking Central Coast, is where the vast expanse of the Pacific Ocean meets the majestic Santa Ynez Mountains. This region, covering approximately 2,774 square miles, is a tapestry of diverse landscapes, ranging from serene beaches to rugged mountainous terrains, all playing a significant role in shaping the culture, lifestyle, and economy of the area.

Major Towns

- **Santa Barbara:** The county seat, known as the "American Riviera," boasts a picturesque Mediterranean flair, with its iconic Spanish colonial architecture. Downtown Santa Barbara, especially along State Street, is vibrant with shops, restaurants, and cultural venues, while the waterfront area is a haven for beach lovers and those seeking leisurely strolls on Stearns Wharf.
- **Goleta:** To the west of Santa Barbara, Goleta offers a blend of natural beauty and innovation, home to high-tech industries propelled by the University of California, Santa Barbara (UCSB). It's also known for the Goleta Butterfly Grove and tranquil Goleta Beach.
- **Solvang:** This charming Danish village in the Santa Ynez Valley is celebrated for its authentic Danish bakeries, architecture, and windmills. Solvang is a gateway to exploring the county's renowned wine culture amid the scenic backdrop of vineyards and rolling hills.
- **Lompoc:** Known for its vibrant flower fields and burgeoning wine industry, Lompoc balances agricultural heritage with the technological advancements of the Vandenberg Space Force Base. It's also home to the historic La Purisima Mission.
- **Santa Maria:** The largest city in the county, Santa Maria, is a focal point for agriculture, particularly noted for its wineries and distinctive barbecue tradition. It serves as an access point to the expansive vineyards

of the Santa Maria Valley and the natural wonders of the Guadalupe-Nipomo Dunes.
- **Carpinteria:** Famous for its gentle beaches, including the world-renowned Rincon Point for surfing, Carpinteria exudes a small-town charm while offering a unique blend of natural beauty, from its seal rookery to lush avocado orchards.
- **Montecito:** Nestled between the mountains and the sea, Montecito is synonymous with luxury and exclusivity. Its well-manicured landscapes, high-end boutiques, and celebrity homes make it a uniquely opulent experience, not to mention the serene beaches and hiking trails.
- **Santa Ynez:** At the heart of the county's wine country, Santa Ynez is surrounded by vineyards and horse ranches, embodying the rustic charm of California's ranching and winemaking heritage. It's also a hub for gourmet dining and historical exploration.

Natural Landmarks

- **Channel Islands National Park:** This park, encompassing five of the Channel Islands, is a pristine natural sanctuary offering adventures like hiking, snorkeling, and unparalleled wildlife viewing. It's a living museum showcasing California's ancient ecosystems.
- **Los Padres National Forest:** Covering the northeastern part of the county, this vast national forest invites outdoor enthusiasts with its extensive trails, camping sites, and breathtaking wilderness areas, including the San Rafael Wilderness.
- **Santa Ynez Mountains:** Providing a dramatic backdrop to the county, these mountains are crisscrossed with trails leading to stunning vistas and historical sites, including the beloved Cold Spring Tavern.
- **Gaviota Coast:** A treasure of undeveloped coastal beauty, the Gaviota Coast features rugged cliffs, hidden beaches, and the iconic Gaviota State Park, representing the quintessence of Southern California's wild shoreline.

Santa Barbara County's geography is a compelling mix of urban elegance and untamed nature, offering a rich palette of experiences for visitors and locals alike. From the culturally rich streets of its towns to the untouched beauty of its natural landmarks, the county embodies the diverse allure of California's Central Coast.

The Climate and Best Times to Visit

Santa Barbara County enjoys a Mediterranean climate, famed for its mild, wet winters and warm, dry summers. This idyllic climate pattern creates a year-round haven for outdoor activities, cultural exploration, and relaxation, making it a desirable destination for travelers with diverse interests. Understanding the nuances of this climate and the area's seasonal offerings can significantly enhance the timing and enjoyment of your visit.

Understanding the Mediterranean Climate

- **Mild Winters:** From December through February, Santa Barbara County experiences a more relaxed and wetter season. However, "cool" is relative, with daytime temperatures typically ranging from the mid-50s to mid-60s Fahrenheit (around 13-18°C), which is relatively mild compared to much of the United States. Rainfall during these months contributes to the lushness of the landscapes, making this an excellent time for those who enjoy green, picturesque settings and don't mind a bit of rain.
- **Warm, Dry Summers:** June through August marks the summer season, where the climate dries, and temperatures warm up, averaging from the high 60s to low 80s Fahrenheit (20-28°C). The warm weather is perfect for beach activities and hiking, as well as the county's many outdoor dining and wine-tasting venues.
- **Pleasant Springs and Falls:** March through May and September through November are particularly appealing visiting times. These transitional seasons feature comfortable temperatures, fewer crowds,

and the natural beauty of the county in bloom during spring and the harvest colors in fall. Spring brings wildflower blooms, especially in the natural parks, while fall is synonymous with the wine harvest season, offering unique experiences in the vineyards and local wineries.

Best Times to Visit Based on Interests

- **For Outdoor Activities:** If you're drawn to outdoor adventures like hiking, surfing, or kayaking, the late spring to early fall (May through September) provides optimal weather conditions. The warmer months allow for comfortable exploration of the county's natural landscapes, from the beaches to the mountains.
- **Cultural and Culinary Exploration:** Those interested in cultural festivals, culinary events, and wine-tasting experiences might find spring and fall the best times to visit. The Santa Barbara International Film Festival, typically held in early spring, and various wine festivals in the fall offer rich cultural experiences with less crowded settings.
- **Beach Vacations:** The summer months are ideal for beachgoers. The warm temperatures and minimal rainfall create perfect conditions for swimming, sunbathing, and beach sports. However, early fall offers warm, pleasant beach days with thinner crowds.
- **Seeking Solitude and Value:** If avoiding crowds and seeking value are your priorities, consider visiting during winter. You'll enjoy lower accommodation rates and the serene beauty of the county's landscapes in their most tranquil state. Winter also brings unique opportunities for whale watching and enjoying the crisp, clear days that follow the rain.

Santa Barbara County's climate and seasonal rhythms offer something special for every visitor, regardless of the time of year. By aligning your visit with your interests and the seasonal characteristics of the region, you can create an unforgettable experience tailored just for you.

3

Santa Barbara: The Heart of The County

Downtown Santa Barbara: Must-Visit Spots and Historical Landmarks

Downtown Santa Barbara is a vibrant heart of the county, where Spanish colonial heritage beautifully intertwines with modern Californian culture. This area is a treasure trove of architectural wonders, lush gardens, and bustling marketplaces, each telling a part of Santa Barbara's rich history and present-day charm. Here's a detailed exploration of must-visit spots and historical landmarks in downtown Santa Barbara.

State Street

- **The Pulse of Downtown:** State Street is the main artery of downtown Santa Barbara, lined with a variety of shops, restaurants, galleries, and theaters. This lively street offers everything from high-end boutiques to independent bookstores, making it a perfect starting point for exploring the area.
- **Architectural Highlights:** As you stroll down State Street, admire the Spanish Revival architecture, characterized by white stucco walls, red-tiled roofs, and ornate ironwork. This style reflects the city's effort to rebuild in the Spanish Colonial style after the devastating 1925

earthquake.

The Santa Barbara County Courthouse

- **A Symbol of Beauty and Justice:** The Santa Barbara County Courthouse is not just a functioning governmental building but also a stunning example of Spanish Colonial Revival architecture. Its elaborate murals, beautiful tiles, and lush gardens make it a must-visit landmark.
- **Sunken Garden and Clock Tower:** The Courthouse's Sunken Garden is an oasis of tranquility, hosting various community events and weddings. Climb the Clock Tower for panoramic views of downtown Santa Barbara and the surrounding mountains.

The Mission Santa Barbara

- **Historical and Spiritual Beacon:** Although slightly removed from the downtown core, the Mission Santa Barbara is an essential part of the city's cultural and historical landscape. Founded in 1786, it's known as the "Queen of the Missions" for its stunning beauty and size.
- **Architectural and Artistic Marvel:** The Mission's complex includes a church, museum, and garden. The church's façade, inspired by Roman architecture, and the meticulously maintained gardens provide insight into the life of the early Spanish settlers and the Native American communities they interacted with.

The Santa Barbara Public Market

- **Culinary Delights:** Located on Victoria Street, near State Street, the Santa Barbara Public Market is a hub for food lovers. This market features an array of local vendors offering everything from artisanal cheeses to craft beer and gourmet chocolates. It's a great place to sample the flavors of the Central Coast.

Paseo Nuevo

- **Shopping and Entertainment:** Paseo Nuevo is an open-air shopping and dining destination in the heart of downtown. Its beautiful Spanish-inspired architecture and courtyards offer a unique shopping experience, complete with boutiques, international brands, and eateries.

The Arlington Theatre

- **Cultural Icon:** The Arlington Theatre serves as both a cinema and a venue for live performances. Its Spanish Colonial architecture and interior designed to mimic a Mediterranean village under a twilight sky make it a fascinating destination for entertainment and architecture enthusiasts alike.

The Lobero Theatre

- **Historic Venue:** The Lobero Theatre is California's oldest, continuously operating theatre. Founded in 1873 and rebuilt in 1924, it showcases the city's commitment to the performing arts. It's a prime venue for jazz concerts, classical performances, and film festivals.

Alice Keck Park Memorial Gardens

- **Nature in the City:** This park is a serene spot featuring a large botanical collection, koi pond, and walking paths. It's an example of the city's dedication to green spaces and provides a peaceful retreat from the urban environment.

Exploring downtown Santa Barbara reveals a city that values its history while embracing the vibrancy of modern life. Each landmark and hidden gem offers a unique perspective on Santa Barbara's cultural richness, making it an essential experience for any visitor to the county.

The Santa Barbara Mission: A Dive into Its History and Present-Day Significance

The Mission Santa Barbara, often called the "Queen of the Missions," stands as a testament to the city's rich colonial past and its enduring cultural and spiritual significance. Founded on December 4, 1786, by Spanish Franciscans, it was the tenth mission established in California, part of a chain of missions aimed at converting the indigenous Chumash people to Christianity and extending Spanish territorial claims. Its history and relevance paint a picture of resilience, cultural integration, and architectural magnificence.

Historical Overview

- **Founding and Purpose:** Padre Fermín Lasuén founded the mission as a continuation of Father Junípero Serra's vision of establishing Spanish missions across California. Its primary goal was to convert the local Chumash people to Christianity, acting as a religious and cultural hub.
- **Architectural Evolution:** The current church, known for its striking façade and twin bell towers, is the fourth iteration, completed in 1820 after earthquakes damaged the previous structures. This structure is a prime example of Spanish Colonial architecture, incorporating elements of Moorish, Byzantine, and Romanesque styles.
- **Economic and Social Hub:** Beyond its religious functions, the Mission was a center for agriculture, education, and craftsmanship. It taught the Chumash various European farming techniques, trades, and arts and played a crucial role in shaping the region's economic landscape.

Present-Day Significance

- **Cultural Heritage Site:** Today, the Mission Santa Barbara serves as a powerful symbol of California's Spanish colonial history, attracting scholars, architects, and visitors from around the world. Its preservation allows for a deeper understanding of the complex interactions between the Spanish colonizers and the native populations.

- **Active Parish and Community Center:** Mission Santa Barbara remains an active parish unlike many historical missions that serve primarily as museums. It hosts regular worship services, weddings, and community events, continuing its centuries-old tradition of serving as a spiritual hub.
- **Educational Resource:** The Mission houses a museum showcasing art, artifacts, and documents related to its history and the Chumash people's daily lives and Spanish settlers' lives. Educational tours and programs offer insights into the Mission's role in California's development and the broader history of Spanish colonization in the Americas.
- **Architectural Marvel:** Preservation efforts ensure that the Mission remains an outstanding example of Spanish Colonial architecture, with its intricately designed façade, beautiful gardens, and historic cemetery. It stands as a beacon of architectural and cultural preservation.
- **Engagement with Indigenous History:** In recent years, there has been a growing emphasis on acknowledging and integrating the history and contributions of the Chumash people both in the Mission's educational programming and in its role as a community center. This effort aims to present a more holistic and respectful view of the region's history.

Impact on Santa Barbara and Beyond

The Mission Santa Barbara's enduring legacy is reflected in its physical presence and its role as a custodian of history, culture, and spirituality. It continues to be a place of reflection, education, and celebration, bridging past and present. For residents and visitors alike, the Mission is a reminder of Santa Barbara's multifaceted identity, shaped by diverse influences and histories. Its ongoing mission to serve as a vibrant community resource while preserving the complex narratives of its past ensures that the "Queen of the Missions" will remain a cherished landmark for generations to come.

Beaches and Parks: A Guide to Enjoying Santa Barbara's Natural Beauty

Santa Barbara, often hailed for its idyllic climate and breathtaking landscapes, is home to some of the most beautiful beaches and parks in California. These natural havens offer a multitude of outdoor activities, from serene beach walks and sunbathing to hiking, picnicking, and wildlife watching in lush parks. Here's an in-depth guide to making the most of Santa Barbara's natural beauty through its beaches and parks.

Beaches

- **East Beach:** As one of Santa Barbara's most popular beaches, East Beach is perfect for volleyball enthusiasts, sunbathers, and families. Its soft sands, picturesque palm trees, and proximity to the Santa Barbara Zoo make it a favorite for both locals and visitors. The beach's Cabrillo Pavilion provides facilities and a beachside restaurant, enhancing the beach day experience.
- **Butterfly Beach:** Located in Montecito, Butterfly Beach faces west, making it an exceptional spot for sunset views. It's a more upscale, quieter beach, favored for sunbathing, dog walking, and celebrity spotting. Its lack of public facilities preserves its tranquil ambiance.
- **Arroyo Burro Beach (Hendry's Beach):** A haven for dog lovers, Arroyo Burro Beach allows off-leash fun in designated areas. Its rugged beauty is complemented by tide pools and cliffside trails. The Boathouse restaurant offers seaside dining, and there are ample facilities for a comfortable day out.
- **Leadbetter Beach:** Popular with beginner surfers, windsurfers, and stand-up paddleboarders, Leadbetter Beach is known for its gentle waves and wide sandy expanse. It's a great spot for picnics and beachside barbecues, with grassy areas, showers, and restrooms available.

Parks

- **Elings Park:** Offering panoramic views of the city and ocean, Elings Park is one of the largest public parks in Santa Barbara. Its vast acreage includes hiking and biking trails, paragliding, soccer fields, and softball diamonds, making it a versatile spot for sports enthusiasts and nature lovers alike.
- **Lotusland:** This internationally renowned botanical garden in Montecito was the private estate of Madame Ganna Walska. Lotusland features an extraordinary collection of exotic plants arranged in stunning gardens, including cacti, bromeliads, and, of course, lotuses. Reservations are required to visit, and the experience is unforgettable.
- **Santa Barbara Botanic Garden:** Dedicated to California native plants, this botanic garden showcases the diverse flora of the region. With over 5 miles of trails, visitors can explore various habitats, including redwood forests, meadows, and desert areas. It's not only a place for relaxation but also education about conservation and native plant landscaping.
- **Shoreline Park:** A gem along the coast, Shoreline Park is a narrow strip of green overlooking the ocean. It's perfect for picnics, jogging, and enjoying unobstructed ocean views. The park includes a playground, picnic areas, and access to a beach below.
- **Alice Keck Park Memorial Gardens:** Known for its peaceful ambiance, Alice Keck Park features a large pond with koi and turtles, a sensory garden with plants selected for their fragrance and texture, and beautifully landscaped areas with a wide variety of plants and trees. It's an ideal spot for a quiet stroll or a serene moment in nature.

Santa Barbara's beaches and parks are integral to the city's charm and appeal, offering endless opportunities to enjoy the outdoors and connect with the natural world. Whether you're seeking adventure, relaxation, or simply a beautiful setting to spend the day, Santa Barbara's natural beauty provides a perfect backdrop for an array of activities suited to every preference.

Dining Choices in Santa Barbara

Joe's Cafe

Joe's Cafe, a historic landmark and the oldest restaurant in Santa Barbara, has been a cornerstone of the city's dining scene since it opened its doors in 1928. Renowned for its hearty American fare, strong cocktails, and vibrant atmosphere, Joe's Cafe has been welcoming guests with open arms for nearly a century, offering a dining experience that blends tradition with the lively spirit of Santa Barbara.

The ambiance of Joe's Cafe is a nod to its rich history, featuring a classic diner-style setup that evokes a sense of nostalgia. The interior is characterized by its vintage decor, including a long, inviting bar, cozy booths, and historic photos that adorn the walls, telling the story of Santa Barbara through the ages. The energy at Joe's is always buzzing, making it a popular spot for both locals and visitors looking for a lively dining experience.

Joe's Cafe prides itself on serving generous portions of classic American dishes, prepared with quality ingredients and a touch of homestyle cooking. The menu features a wide range of options, from juicy burgers and succulent steaks to fresh salads and hearty breakfasts served all day. Signature dishes include the Joe's Special, a satisfying scramble of eggs, ground beef, spinach, and onions, and the Prime Rib dinner, a weekend favorite that draws crowds from all over.

What sets Joe's Cafe apart, aside from its delicious food, is its legendary bar. Known for serving some of the strongest drinks in town, Joe's has become a go-to spot for those looking to enjoy a lively night out. The cocktail menu features a mix of classic and contemporary drinks, all poured with a generous hand.

Joe's Cafe is more than just a restaurant; it's a part of Santa Barbara's history and a gathering place where memories are made. Whether you're stopping by for a hearty breakfast, enjoying a casual lunch, or kicking off a night on the town with dinner and drinks, Joe's Cafe offers a warm welcome and an unforgettable experience that captures the essence of Santa Barbara's dining culture.

Holdren's Steak House

Holdren's Steak House, a staple in the Santa Barbara dining landscape, epitomizes the classic American steakhouse experience. It marries the timeless charm of traditional steakhouse cuisine with the laid-back elegance of the California coast. Known for its exceptional cuts of meat, cozy ambiance, and impeccable service, Holdren's has established itself as a prime destination for both locals and visitors craving a top-notch steak dinner.

The atmosphere at Holdren's Steak House is intimate and welcoming. It features rich wood paneling, soft lighting, and comfortable seating that invite guests to relax and indulge. The restaurant's interior exudes a classic steakhouse feel, with a touch of sophistication that reflects the upscale yet unpretentious vibe of Santa Barbara. Whether dining in the main room or enjoying a drink at the bar, guests at Holdren's are treated to a warm and convivial dining experience.

At the heart of Holdren's menu is a selection of premium steaks, each hand-cut and expertly grilled to perfection. From the succulent filet mignon to the robust New York strip, every steak is seasoned and cooked to the diner's specifications, ensuring a flawless steakhouse experience. Beyond steaks, Holdren's offers a variety of seafood dishes, hearty salads, and classic sides, such as the creamy garlic mashed potatoes and the sautéed mushrooms, all prepared with the same attention to quality and flavor.

Holdren's Steak House also boasts an impressive wine list, featuring a range of local Santa Barbara wines alongside national and international selections, carefully chosen to complement the rich flavors of the menu. The bar serves up classic cocktails, premium spirits, and craft beers, providing plenty of options for pairing or enjoying a drink in good company.

Holdren's Steak House is more than just a place to eat; it's a dining destination that celebrates the art of the steak dinner. Whether marking a special occasion, hosting a business dinner, or simply treating oneself to an exquisite meal, Holdren's offers an experience that combines the best of traditional steakhouse fare with the unique charm of Santa Barbara's culinary scene.

The Lark Santa Barbara

The Lark Santa Barbara, located in the heart of the city's vibrant Funk Zone neighborhood, is a culinary gem that epitomizes the spirit of community and shared dining. This award-winning restaurant is celebrated for its innovative approach to contemporary American cuisine, strongly emphasizing seasonal and locally sourced ingredients. The Lark's menu is a reflection of the rich agricultural and coastal bounty of California's Central Coast, offering dishes that are both inventive and deeply rooted in the area's culinary traditions.

Upon entering The Lark, diners are greeted with a beautifully designed space combining industrial chic and rustic elegance. The restaurant's interior, featuring reclaimed wood, vintage decor, and eclectic lighting, creates a warm, inviting, sophisticated, and relaxed atmosphere. The expansive outdoor patio, adorned with fire pits and communal tables, provides an ideal setting for al fresco dining under the Santa Barbara sky.

The Lark's menu is designed for sharing, encouraging diners to experience a variety of flavors and textures. Each dish is meticulously prepared and beautifully presented, from small plates and artisanal charcuterie to hearty main courses and inventive sides. Signature items include the market fish, prepared with seasonal accompaniments, and the famous Lark Burger, a gourmet take on the classic American burger.

The Lark's commitment to excellence extends to its beverage program, which features an extensive selection of local wines, craft beers, and artisanal cocktails. Inspired by the local flora and fauna, the cocktail menu offers unique and refreshing drinks that perfectly complement the dining experience.

Dining at The Lark Santa Barbara is not just a meal; it's an occasion to savor the best of California's culinary offerings in a setting that celebrates the joy of sharing good food with good company. Whether you're a local or a visitor, The Lark promises an unforgettable dining experience that captures the essence of Santa Barbara's casual sophistication and innovative spirit.

Loquita

Loquita, a standout culinary destination in Santa Barbara's Funk Zone, pays homage to the rich flavors and vibrant spirit of Spain. Specializing in authentic Spanish cuisine, Loquita showcases the traditional tapas culture, paellas, and wood-fired grilled meats and seafood, complemented by a meticulously curated selection of Spanish wines and innovative cocktails. The restaurant's commitment to authenticity and quality ingredients transports diners to the bustling streets of Barcelona or the charming plazas of Sevilla.

The ambiance at Loquita matches the warmth and passion of its cuisine. The interior is beautifully adorned with Spanish tiles, rustic wood, and touches of greenery, creating a cozy yet sophisticated setting. Outdoor dining is equally enchanting, offering a lively patio space where guests can enjoy the mild Santa Barbara evenings under string lights, adding to the overall Mediterranean experience.

Loquita's menu celebrates Spain's diverse regional cuisines, expertly prepared with a contemporary twist. The tapas selection invites diners to embark on a culinary journey, featuring everything from Jamón Ibérico and Manchego cheese to gambas al ajillo (garlic shrimp) and patatas bravas. The paellas, cooked in traditional shallow pans, are a not-to-be-missed highlight, offering a communal dining experience that's at the heart of Spanish culture.

The bar at Loquita serves an impressive array of Spanish wines, focusing on both well-known regions and hidden gems, alongside sherries, vermouths, and cava. The cocktail menu draws inspiration from Spanish ingredients and traditions, featuring creative concoctions that perfectly complement the bold flavors of the food.

Loquita is more than just a restaurant; it's a vibrant celebration of Spanish gastronomy and culture. Whether you're sharing a selection of tapas among friends, enjoying a romantic dinner for two, or toasting with sangria on the patio, Loquita offers an unforgettable dining experience that captures the essence of Spain in the heart of Santa Barbara.

Brophy Bros. Clam Bar & Restaurant

Brophy Bros. Clam Bar & Restaurant, perched on the edge of Santa Barbara's picturesque harbor, offers a quintessential seaside dining experience that locals and visitors alike have cherished for years. Brophy Bros. embodies the spirit of coastal California dining, renowned for its fresh seafood, lively atmosphere, and breathtaking views of the marina and the Santa Ynez Mountains.

The ambiance at Brophy Bros. is casual and bustling, with an open-air bar and dining area that invites diners to soak in the vibrant harbor life. The restaurant's interior is adorned with nautical decor, from fishing nets to vintage maritime artifacts, enhancing the authentic seafood shack vibe. Large windows and outdoor seating ensure that every seat in the house boasts a stunning view, making it a prime location for watching boats glide by or catching a spectacular sunset over the Pacific.

The menu at Brophy Bros. focuses on the bounty of the sea, offering an array of fresh seafood dishes prepared with simplicity and flair. The clam bar features freshly shucked oysters, steamed clams, and mussels, served with Brophy Bros.' signature sourdough bread, perfect for sopping up delicious broths and sauces. The restaurant's clam chowder, rich and creamy, has garnered a loyal following, while the fish and chips, crispy and golden, are a nod to classic seafood fare.

Brophy Bros. is also known for its generous portions and selection of local beers and wines, complementing the seafood-centric menu. The convivial bar area becomes a lively gathering spot, where guests can enjoy a cold beer or a glass of Santa Barbara wine, adding to the restaurant's festive atmosphere.

Whether you're in the mood for a leisurely lunch after exploring the harbor, a casual dinner with family and friends, or simply a refreshing drink with a view, Brophy Bros. Clam Bar & Restaurant offers a memorable dining experience. Its combination of fresh seafood, stunning scenery, and a warm, welcoming atmosphere captures the essence of Santa Barbara's seaside charm.

Bouchon Santa Barbara

Bouchon Santa Barbara is a culinary jewel in the heart of downtown, celebrating the abundance of flavors and ingredients found in California's Central Coast region. This elegant restaurant is dedicated to bringing the French bistro experience to Santa Barbara, focusing on farm-to-table dining that highlights the best local produce, meats, and seafood. Bouchon's commitment to quality and sustainability is evident in every dish, offering diners a truly authentic taste of the area's culinary bounty.

The atmosphere at Bouchon is warm and inviting, featuring cozy dining spaces adorned with soft lighting and rustic decor that evoke the charm of a French country inn. The intimate setting is perfect for special occasions, romantic dinners, or anyone looking to indulge in a gourmet meal in a relaxed yet refined environment. During warmer months, the outdoor patio becomes a delightful space to enjoy a meal under the stars, surrounded by the gentle buzz of the city.

Bouchon's menu is a testament to the richness of Santa Barbara's agriculture and viticulture, skillfully blending traditional French techniques with the vibrant flavors of the West Coast. Signature dishes include the locally sourced duck breast, perfectly seared and served with a seasonal fruit compote, and the Pacific halibut, expertly prepared and accompanied by a melody of farm-fresh vegetables. Each dish is thoughtfully paired with wines from the extensive list that features selections from Santa Barbara's premier wineries, enhancing the dining experience with exquisite flavors and aromas.

The service at Bouchon is attentive and knowledgeable, with staff eager to share the stories behind the menu's offerings and assist with wine pairings, ensuring that every meal is both delicious and educational. The restaurant's dedication to creating memorable dining experiences is evident in the meticulous attention to detail, from the food's presentation to the dining room's ambiance.

Dining at Bouchon Santa Barbara is not just a meal; it's an exploration of the Central Coast's culinary landscape, presented with elegance and passion. Whether you're a local food enthusiast or a visitor looking to taste the best of what Santa Barbara has to offer, Bouchon provides a sophisticated yet approachable venue for savoring the flavors of the region in true French bistro style.

Olio e Limone Ristorante

Olio e Limone Ristorante, nestled in the heart of downtown Santa Barbara, is a bastion of Italian culinary excellence, where tradition meets sophistication in an elegant yet comfortable setting. The name, translating to "Oil and Lemon," reflects the restaurant's commitment to simplicity and quality, emphasizing the pure flavors of meticulously sourced ingredients. Olio e Limone provides an authentic Italian dining experience, offering a menu that travels through Italy's rich culinary landscapes, from the rolling hills of Tuscany to the vibrant streets of Sicily.

The ambiance at Olio e Limone is refined and inviting, featuring crisp white tablecloths, soft lighting, and an understated decor that allows the food to take center stage. The intimate dining room creates an atmosphere of warmth and hospitality, making it ideal for romantic dinners, special celebrations, or business meetings. The attention to detail in the service and presentation elevates the dining experience, ensuring that every guest feels welcomed and cherished.

The menu at Olio e Limone showcases the breadth of Italian cuisine, with dishes prepared with an unwavering dedication to authenticity and flavor. Starters such as the carpaccio di manzo, thinly sliced raw beef drizzled with lemon-infused olive oil, set the stage for a culinary journey. Pasta dishes, like the handmade pappardelle with wild boar ragù, exemplify the restaurant's artisanal approach, while main courses, such as the branzino al limone, highlight the freshness of the sea.

Olio e Limone's wine list is a carefully curated selection of Italian wines, chosen to complement the flavors of the menu and introduce diners to the diverse wine regions of Italy. The knowledgeable staff are on hand to recommend perfect pairings, enhancing the meal with the ideal accompaniment to each dish.

Beyond the exquisite cuisine, Olio e Limone is committed to creating an experience that reflects the joy and passion of Italian dining. The restaurant often hosts special events, wine dinners, and tasting menus that celebrate the culinary traditions of Italy, inviting guests to immerse themselves in the rich flavors and festive spirit of Italian cuisine.

Dining at Olio e Limone Ristorante is more than just a meal; it's a journey to the heart of Italy, where every dish is prepared with love and every bite tells a story of tradition, quality, and culinary excellence. Whether you're a connoisseur of Italian cuisine or simply seeking a memorable dining experience in Santa Barbara, Olio e Limone promises an evening of delightful flavors, warm hospitality, and the timeless charm of Italy.

Mesa Verde

Mesa Verde, nestled in the heart of Santa Barbara, is a groundbreaking restaurant that redefines plant-based dining with its inventive and globally inspired cuisine. This restaurant is a haven for those seeking a vegetarian or vegan culinary experience that doesn't compromise on flavor, creativity, or presentation. Mesa Verde has garnered a loyal following among both plant-based diners and omnivores alike, thanks to its commitment to fresh, organic ingredients and its ability to transform them into extraordinary dishes.

The ambiance of Mesa Verde is as vibrant and refreshing as its menu. The interior boasts a contemporary and artistic design, with natural light flooding in to illuminate the earthy, minimalist decor. The dining space is adorned with lush plants and rustic elements, creating a serene and welcoming environment that reflects the restaurant's connection to nature. Outdoor seating is available, offering a delightful al fresco dining experience in Santa Barbara's picturesque setting.

Mesa Verde's menu is a celebration of plant-based cuisine, showcasing the versatility and richness of vegetables, grains, and legumes through a variety of dishes that draw inspiration from around the world. Signature dishes include innovative takes on classics, such as the black bean burger served with a side of sweet potato fries, and more adventurous creations like the jackfruit tacos, which are a hit for their meaty texture and robust flavor. The restaurant also offers a selection of raw dishes, nourishing bowls, and decadent desserts, ensuring there's something to satisfy every craving.

The beverage program at Mesa Verde complements the dining experience with a selection of organic wines, craft beers, and inventive cocktails made with fresh juices and botanicals. The restaurant also offers a variety of house-made kombuchas and herbal teas, emphasizing wellness and natural flavors.

Mesa Verde is more than just a restaurant; it's a culinary destination that invites diners to explore the depth and breadth of plant-based cuisine in an environment that celebrates creativity, sustainability, and the joy of eating well. Whether you're a devoted vegan or simply curious about plant-based dining, Mesa Verde promises a memorable meal that delights the senses and nourishes the body.

Santa Barbara Shellfish Company

Perched at the very end of Stearns Wharf with unparalleled views of the Pacific Ocean, the Santa Barbara Shellfish Company started its journey as a simple fishermen's bait and tackle shop that eventually evolved into one of Santa Barbara's most cherished seafood destinations. This establishment is a true homage to the ocean's bounty, specializing in fresh shellfish and seafood dishes that capture the essence of coastal dining.

The ambiance of the Santa Barbara Shellfish Company is unpretentious and welcoming, with a bustling, open kitchen and casual seating that allows diners to immerse themselves in the sights and sounds of the harbor. The restaurant's modest size and oceanfront location offer an intimate dining experience, where the focus is squarely on the food and the spectacular maritime views. Guests can enjoy their meals indoors or opt for outdoor seating on the wharf for a closer connection to the sea.

The menu at the Santa Barbara Shellfish Company is a seafood lover's delight, featuring an array of freshly caught shellfish and fish prepared with minimal fuss to highlight their natural flavors. Signature dishes include the Santa Barbara uni (sea urchin), sourced directly from local waters and served fresh, the succulent lobster tacos, and the famous shellfish platter, which offers a sampling of the day's best catches. The restaurant also boasts a selection of freshly shucked oysters, clams, and mussels, along with heartier options like the Dungeness crab and spiny lobster, depending on the season.

True to its roots, the Santa Barbara Shellfish Company maintains a close relationship with local fishermen, ensuring that the seafood on offer is fresh and sustainably harvested. This commitment to quality and sustainability extends to the restaurant's selection of wines and beers, carefully chosen to complement the seafood-centric menu.

Dining at the Santa Barbara Shellfish Company is a quintessential Santa

Barbara experience, offering a taste of the ocean's freshest flavors in a setting that is as unassuming as it is beautiful. Whether you're stopping by for a quick lunch or settling in for a leisurely dinner against the backdrop of a stunning sunset, this establishment promises a memorable meal that celebrates the simple pleasures of fresh seafood and good company.

Santo Mezcal

Nestled in the heart of Santa Barbara's vibrant downtown, Santo Mezcal stands out as a culinary beacon celebrating contemporary Mexican cuisine's rich flavors and traditions. This restaurant is a testament to the complexity and diversity of Mexico's gastronomic heritage, offering a modern interpretation that is both innovative and deeply rooted in tradition. Santo Mezcal has quickly become a favorite among locals and visitors alike, drawn to its sophisticated menu, stylish ambiance, and commitment to showcasing the finest ingredients.

The interior of Santo Mezcal exudes urban chic, with a sleek and modern design that incorporates elements of Mexican art and culture. The dining space is both elegant and inviting, creating an atmosphere that is perfect for intimate dinners, casual lunches, or celebratory gatherings. An outdoor patio offers al fresco dining, allowing guests to enjoy Santa Barbara's idyllic weather alongside their meal.

Santo Mezcal's menu is a vibrant mosaic of flavors, with each dish thoughtfully crafted to highlight the quality and freshness of its ingredients. The restaurant specializes in artisanal mezcal and tequila, which are expertly paired with the menu items to enhance the dining experience. Signature dishes include succulent seafood offerings like the grilled octopus served with a smoky mezcal sauce, and the innovative aguachile, which marries the freshness of raw fish with the bright acidity of citrus and the heat of chilies.

The restaurant also offers a variety of handcrafted cocktails that draw on traditional Mexican spirits and flavors, incorporating fresh, local produce to create drinks that are as visually stunning as they are delicious. The Santo Mezcal cocktail, featuring mezcal, agave nectar, and fresh lime, is a must-try, perfectly encapsulating the restaurant's ethos of simplicity and excellence.

Santo Mezcal's dedication to creating an exceptional dining experience extends to its service. Knowledgeable staff is ready to guide guests through the menu and offer recommendations on food and drink pairings. This commitment to hospitality and the restaurant's innovative approach to Mexican cuisine make Santo Mezcal a standout destination in Santa Barbara's culinary scene.

Dining at Santo Mezcal is not just a meal; it's an exploration of Mexico's rich culinary landscape, presented with a modern flair that respects tradition and is eager to push boundaries. Whether you're a connoisseur of Mexican cuisine or simply looking to enjoy a meal that is as memorable as it is flavorful, Santo Mezcal promises an experience that will captivate your senses and leave you eager to return.

Arigato Sushi

Arigato Sushi stands as a beacon of culinary excellence in Santa Barbara, offering an innovative and exquisite take on Japanese cuisine that transcends the traditional sushi dining experience. Nestled in the bustling heart of the city, this restaurant has cultivated a reputation for its creative sushi rolls, sashimi, and Japanese dishes, all crafted from the freshest ingredients and presented with artistic flair.

The ambiance of Arigato Sushi combines modern sophistication with the warm, welcoming essence of traditional Japanese design. The interior features sleek, contemporary decor with subtle Asian influences, creating an elegant yet comfortable dining environment. The sushi bar is a focal point, where guests can watch as skilled chefs prepare their meals with precision and artistry. The restaurant also offers table seating, providing an intimate setting for diners to enjoy their meals.

Arigato Sushi's menu is a testament to the diversity and richness of Japanese cuisine, featuring a wide range of options that cater to various tastes and preferences. Signature rolls like the Dragon Roll and the Arigato Roll demonstrate the chefs' creativity, blending flavors and textures in unexpected ways. In addition to sushi, the restaurant serves an array of traditional

Japanese dishes, including tempura, teriyaki, and udon, ensuring there's something for everyone.

The quality of the seafood at Arigato Sushi is unmatched, with the restaurant sourcing its fish from the best suppliers to guarantee freshness and flavor. This commitment to quality extends to the restaurant's selection of sake and Japanese beers, curated to complement the dishes and enhance the dining experience.

Dining at Arigato Sushi is not merely a meal; it's an exploration of the nuanced flavors and exquisite presentation that define Japanese cuisine. Whether you're a sushi aficionado or new to Japanese food, Arigato Sushi promises a memorable dining experience that combines the best of tradition and innovation in the heart of Santa Barbara.

Los Agaves

Los Agaves, a family-owned gem, has quickly risen to become one of Santa Barbara's most beloved Mexican restaurants, renowned for its vibrant flavors, generous portions, and warm, inviting atmosphere. Situated conveniently on the bustling streets of Santa Barbara, Los Agaves offers a culinary journey through Mexico with its authentic dishes that celebrate the rich diversity of Mexican cuisine.

The ambiance at Los Agaves is colorful and lively, reflecting the spirit of Mexican culture with its bright decor and rustic touches. The restaurant creates a welcoming environment where families, friends, and food enthusiasts gather to enjoy high-quality, traditional Mexican meals in a casual and friendly setting. The open kitchen concept allows diners to witness the magic of their meals being prepared, adding to the authentic dining experience.

Los Agaves stands out for its extensive menu that goes beyond the typical fare, offering a variety of regional specialties and innovative dishes that showcase the complexity of Mexican cuisine. Signature dishes include the Mole Oaxaqueño, a rich and aromatic sauce served over tender chicken, and the Enchiladas Suizas, filled with succulent meat and topped with a creamy, tomatillo sauce. The restaurant is also famous for its seafood offerings, such as the Ceviche De La Casa, made with fresh, local seafood marinated in lime juice and spices.

One of the highlights of dining at Los Agaves is the salsa bar, featuring an assortment of homemade salsas ranging from mild to fiery, allowing guests to customize their dishes to their taste preferences. This attention to detail and dedication to authenticity is what sets Los Agaves apart.

The beverage selection at Los Agaves includes traditional Mexican drinks such as horchata and tamarindo, as well as a variety of beers and tequilas, perfect for pairing with the bold flavors of the food.

Los Agaves has not only become a go-to spot for locals seeking authentic Mexican cuisine but also a culinary destination for visitors to Santa Barbara. The combination of delicious, meticulously prepared dishes, a welcoming atmosphere, and attentive service makes dining at Los Agaves a memorable experience that captures the essence of Mexican hospitality and culinary excellence.

The Boathouse at Hendry's Beach

The Boathouse at Hendry's Beach is a quintessential Santa Barbara dining destination, offering an unmatched blend of stunning ocean views, fresh seafood, and a relaxed, coastal atmosphere. Perched directly on the sands of Hendry's Beach, also known as Arroyo Burro Beach, this beloved restaurant provides a dining experience that is as much about the breathtaking scenery as it is about the exquisite food and drink.

Upon arrival, diners are greeted by the sight of the expansive Pacific Ocean and the soothing sounds of waves crashing against the shore. The Boathouse's design maximizes its spectacular location, with ample outdoor seating and large windows ensuring that every guest can enjoy the view. The interior echoes the natural beauty of its surroundings, with a nautical theme that includes wood accents and maritime decor, creating a warm and welcoming environment.

The menu at The Boathouse at Hendry's Beach focuses on seafood, with dishes designed to showcase the freshest catches from local waters. Signature offerings include the grilled wild-caught salmon, served with a seasonal accompaniment, and the Boathouse Cioppino, a rich and hearty seafood stew that's perfect for cooler evenings. The restaurant also serves a variety of breakfast and brunch items, making it a popular morning destination for both locals and visitors eager to start their day with a view.

In addition to its focus on seafood, The Boathouse offers selections for land lovers, including salads, burgers, and steaks, all prepared with the same commitment to quality and flavor. The bar serves a thoughtful selection of local wines and craft beers, alongside signature cocktails that are ideal for sipping as the sun sets over the ocean.

The Boathouse at Hendry's Beach is not just a restaurant; it's an experience. It's a place where couples come for romantic dinners, families gather for celebratory meals, and friends meet for happy hour drinks, all against the backdrop of one of Santa Barbara's most stunning natural landscapes. Whether you're there to dine on the outdoor patio, enjoy a cocktail by the fire pit, or simply relax with a cup of coffee in the morning mist, The Boathouse at Hendry's Beach offers a memorable escape that epitomizes the laid-back luxury of Santa Barbara's coastal lifestyle.

Toma Restaurant & Bar

Toma Restaurant & Bar, nestled along Santa Barbara's picturesque waterfront, is celebrated for its exquisite Italian cuisine and captivating views of the Pacific Ocean. This beloved dining destination offers a warm and inviting atmosphere, where guests can enjoy a sophisticated yet relaxed dining experience. Toma has garnered a reputation for its innovative dishes that blend classic Italian flavors with the freshest local ingredients, creating a menu that is both familiar and exciting.

The ambiance at Toma Restaurant & Bar strikes the perfect balance between elegance and comfort, with its tastefully decorated interior that features rich wood accents, soft lighting, and intimate seating arrangements. The outdoor patio, overlooking the marina, provides a serene setting for dining under the stars, where the gentle sea breeze and the sound of the waves enhance the overall experience.

Toma's menu is a testament to the culinary team's dedication to quality and creativity, offering a range of dishes that cater to diverse tastes and dietary preferences. Signature starters include the Burrata Caprese, featuring creamy burrata cheese paired with heirloom tomatoes and basil pesto, and the Calamari Fritti, lightly fried and served with a spicy aioli. The entrees are a highlight, with standout dishes such as the Ravioli di Aragosta, filled with succulent lobster and served in a rich saffron cream sauce, and the Bistecca Fiorentina. This perfectly grilled steak showcases the quality of the meat.

The wine list at Toma is carefully curated to complement the menu, featuring a wide selection of local Santa Barbara wines alongside Italian classics, allowing guests to explore the depth and variety of both regions. The bar also offers a range of inventive cocktails and premium spirits, making it a popular spot for both pre-dinner drinks and leisurely nightcaps.

Toma Restaurant & Bar is more than just a meal; it's a dining experience that captures the essence of Santa Barbara's culinary scene. It's a place where every visit promises not only a feast for the senses but also a warm, welcoming atmosphere that makes guests feel right at home. Whether you're celebrating a special occasion, enjoying a romantic dinner, or simply treating yourself to a night out, Toma Restaurant & Bar delivers unforgettable moments that linger long after the last bite.

Handlebar Coffee Roasters

Handlebar Coffee Roasters, nestled in the heart of Santa Barbara, stands as a beacon for coffee enthusiasts and casual café-goers alike, epitomizing the city's vibrant coffee culture. Founded by former professional cyclists who turned their passion for coffee into a thriving business, Handlebar has become synonymous with quality, community, and sustainability. Their dedication to sourcing the finest beans from ethical producers around the world, and roasting them to perfection on-site, ensures that every cup served is a testament to their craft.

The ambiance of Handlebar Coffee Roasters is both inviting and dynamic, reflecting the spirit of its founders and the community it serves. The café boasts a minimalist yet cozy interior, with natural light flooding in to highlight the warm wood accents and the gleaming espresso machines. Outdoor seating is available, providing a perfect spot for enjoying a cup of coffee in Santa Barbara's idyllic climate. The atmosphere is always buzzing with the energy of locals meeting for business, friends gathering for leisure, and coffee aficionados engaging in lively discussions about the latest brews.

Handlebar's menu offers an impressive range of coffee drinks, from classic espressos and lattes to seasonal specialties crafted with house-made syrups and alternative milks. Each drink is prepared with precision and care, ensuring the natural flavors of the coffee are front and center. Beyond coffee, the café serves a selection of freshly baked pastries, light bites, and healthier options, all sourced from local producers and bakeries to complement the beverages.

What sets Handlebar Coffee Roasters apart is not just their exceptional coffee but their commitment to the community and the environment. They regularly host events, workshops, and art exhibits, fostering a sense of connection and creativity among Santa Barbara's residents. Their sustainability efforts, from compostable packaging to supporting fair trade practices, reflect a deep respect for the planet and the people who cultivate their coffee.

Visiting Handlebar Coffee Roasters is an experience that goes beyond enjoying a great cup of coffee; it's about being part of a community that values quality, sustainability, and the simple pleasure of sharing good times over great coffee. Whether you're a local or just passing through, Handlebar invites you to pause, savor the moment, and enjoy the best of what Santa Barbara's coffee scene has to offer.

Jeannine's Restaurant & Bakery

Jeannine's Restaurant & Bakery has been a staple in the Santa Barbara dining scene for decades, cherished by locals and visitors for its cozy atmosphere, exceptional breakfast and brunch offerings, and delectable bakery treats. Nestled in the heart of Santa Barbara, Jeannine's presents a welcoming, family-friendly environment where every meal feels like a special occasion, served with a side of genuine hospitality.

The ambiance of Jeannine's is charming and inviting, with a décor that combines rustic elements with a touch of elegance, creating a space that's both sophisticated and comfortable. The restaurant's interior exudes warmth, making guests feel right at home, while the outdoor seating provides a lovely option for those wishing to enjoy their meal al fresco in Santa Barbara's idyllic weather.

Jeannine's menu is renowned for its diverse and flavorful breakfast, brunch, and lunch selections, emphasizing fresh, locally sourced ingredients and inventive twists on classic dishes. Favorites include the fluffy buttermilk pancakes, served with a variety of toppings and syrups; the Eggs Benedict, featuring perfectly poached eggs on homemade English muffins; and the Santa Barbara omelet, filled with avocado, bacon, tomato, and Swiss cheese. The bakery section tempts with an array of freshly baked bread, pastries, and sweets, including their famous scones, muffins, and the decadent banana cream pie.

In addition to the stellar food, Jeannine's offers a selection of coffee beverages, teas, and fresh juices, making it a perfect spot for a morning pick-me-up or a leisurely brunch with friends and family. The attention to detail in every dish and drink, combined with the warm, attentive service, ensures a dining experience that is both satisfying and memorable.

Jeannine's Restaurant & Bakery is more than just a place to eat; it's a beloved community gathering spot where guests can expect to find delicious food, a welcoming atmosphere, and the comforting feeling of being part of the Santa Barbara family. Whether you're starting your day with a hearty breakfast, enjoying a leisurely brunch, or stopping by for a sweet treat from the bakery, Jeannine's promises a delightful experience that captures the essence of casual, coastal dining.

McConnell's Fine Ice Creams

McConnell's Fine Ice Creams, a beloved institution in Santa Barbara since its inception in 1949, stands as a testament to the art of ice cream making. With a legacy spanning over seven decades, McConnell's has set the standard

SANTA BARBARA: THE HEART OF THE COUNTY

for premium ice creams, offering an array of flavors that are rich, creamy, and crafted from the finest ingredients. The dedication to quality and tradition has made McConnell's a favorite among locals and visitors alike, embodying the spirit of Santa Barbara's culinary excellence.

The McConnell's experience begins the moment you step into one of their charming scoop shops, where the vintage-inspired decor and welcoming ambiance invite you to indulge in a moment of pure joy. The shops, designed with a nod to the brand's rich history, offer a delightful space where families, friends, and ice cream lovers of all ages can gather to enjoy a scoop (or two) of their exceptional ice cream.

At the heart of McConnell's Fine Ice Creams is their commitment to using only the best ingredients, including grass-fed milk and cream from local farms, organic eggs, and sustainably sourced chocolates, fruits, and nuts. This commitment ensures that each flavor not only tastes extraordinary but also supports local agriculture and sustainable practices. From classic favorites like Dutch Chocolate and Mint Chip to innovative creations such as Eureka Lemon & Marionberries and Turkish Coffee, McConnell's menu boasts a flavor for every palate.

What sets McConnell's apart is not just the quality of their ice creams but also the innovation behind their flavors. The team continually experiments with unique combinations and seasonal ingredients, resulting in a constantly evolving menu that surprises and delights customers. Their dairy-free options, made from house-made bases of macadamia nuts and coconut oil, ensure that everyone can enjoy the McConnell's experience, regardless of dietary preferences.

Visiting McConnell's Fine Ice Creams is more than just enjoying a dessert; it's about participating in a tradition that has brought joy to generations of Santa Barbarans and visitors. It's a place where the simple pleasure of eating ice cream is elevated to an art form, and where every scoop is a reminder of the care, craftsmanship, and community spirit that defines McConnell's. Whether you're a longtime fan or discovering their flavors for the first time, McConnell's promises an unforgettable ice cream experience that's deeply rooted in the heart of Santa Barbara.

The Santa Barbara Wine Collective

The Santa Barbara Wine Collective is a unique and pioneering establishment in the heart of Santa Barbara's Funk Zone, embodying the collaborative spirit and exceptional viticulture of the Central Coast region. This innovative venue offers an immersive wine-tasting experience, showcasing a curated selection of wines from some of the area's most esteemed and innovative winemakers. It stands as a testament to the diversity and quality of Santa Barbara County's wine country, providing both connoisseurs and casual enthusiasts with a distinctive opportunity to explore the region's vinicultural bounty under one roof.

The ambiance of the Santa Barbara Wine Collective is both sophisticated and welcoming, with a design that blends modern aesthetics with elements reflective of the local winemaking tradition. The space is open and airy, featuring natural light, reclaimed wood, and a minimalist decor that allows the wines to take center stage. Guests can choose to savor their selections at the elegant tasting bar, communal tables, or on the outdoor patio, which offers a relaxed setting perfect for enjoying a glass of wine in the mild Santa Barbara climate.

The collective's wine list is thoughtfully composed, featuring a rotating selection of offerings from member wineries, each chosen for their commitment to quality, sustainability, and expression of terroir. This model allows guests to sample a wide range of varietals and styles, from crisp, refreshing whites and rosés to complex, full-bodied reds. The knowledgeable staff are passionate about wine and eager to share stories about the winemakers, the winemaking process, and the characteristics of each wine, enhancing the tasting experience with their expertise.

In addition to wine tastings, the Santa Barbara Wine Collective offers educational events, winemaker dinners, and private tastings, providing deeper insights into the winemaking process and the unique qualities of the Santa Barbara wine region. These events foster a sense of community among wine lovers and offer an unparalleled opportunity to engage directly with the people behind the wines.

The Santa Barbara Wine Collective is not just a destination for wine tasting;

it's a vibrant hub for the local wine community and a must-visit for anyone looking to experience the best of Santa Barbara's wine culture. Whether you're a seasoned aficionado seeking to expand your palate or a newcomer eager to explore the world of wine, the collective offers a welcoming and enriching experience that celebrates the rich tapestry of Central Coast winemaking.

Scarlett Begonia

Scarlett Begonia, nestled in the charming heart of Santa Barbara, has quickly become a beacon of culinary innovation and a beloved gathering place for those who cherish unique, farm-to-table dining experiences. This restaurant's commitment to sustainability, exceptional quality, and the creative use of seasonal ingredients sets it apart in Santa Barbara's vibrant food scene. Scarlett Begonia offers a thoughtful and adventurous menu, blending classic techniques with modern culinary creativity.

The ambiance of Scarlett Begonia reflects its commitment to comfort and sustainability, featuring a cozy and inviting interior with touches of rustic elegance. The outdoor seating area provides a tranquil oasis for dining al fresco, surrounded by lush greenery and the gentle buzz of the city. Whether you're settling in for a leisurely brunch or enjoying a dinner under the stars, the restaurant offers a warm and welcoming atmosphere that encourages guests to relax and savor the moment.

Scarlett Begonia's menu is a testament to the art of seasonal cooking, with dishes that highlight the freshest local produce, meats, and seafood. The restaurant is particularly renowned for its breakfast and brunch offerings, which include innovative dishes such as lemon ricotta pancakes, savory breakfast bowls, and a variety of artisanal baked goods that are made in-house daily. Lunch and dinner menus evolve with the seasons, featuring inventive salads, hearty entrees, and exquisite small plates that are perfect for sharing.

A standout feature of Scarlett Begonia is its commitment to sourcing ingredients from local farms and producers, ensuring that each dish tastes exceptional and supports the community and the environment. This farm-to-table philosophy extends to the beverage menu, including craft cocktails made with organic spirits and fresh juices, local wines, and artisanal beers.

Scarlett Begonia is more than just a restaurant; it's a culinary destination that celebrates Santa Barbara's bounty and the creativity of its culinary team. The restaurant's dedication to quality, sustainability, and innovation is evident in every bite, making it a must-visit for anyone seeking an unforgettable dining experience in Santa Barbara. Whether you're a local food enthusiast or a visitor exploring the city's culinary delights, Scarlett Begonia promises a meal that is both nourishing for the body and inspiring for the soul.

Jane Restaurant

Jane Restaurant is a cherished culinary landmark in Santa Barbara, renowned for its consistent delivery of exceptional cuisine, warm atmosphere, and attentive service. Situated in a prime location that's easily accessible for both locals and visitors, Jane Restaurant has cemented its reputation as a go-to destination for those seeking a memorable dining experience. The restaurant is named after its owner, providing a personal touch that extends throughout the dining experience, from the carefully curated menu to the welcoming environment.

The ambiance of Jane Restaurant strikes a perfect balance between elegance and comfort, creating an inviting space where guests can enjoy lunch or dinner. The interior boasts a classic design with contemporary touches, featuring rich wood finishes, soft lighting, and tastefully chosen artwork that adds character and charm. The outdoor seating area offers a delightful al fresco dining experience, allowing guests to soak in the Santa Barbara sunshine or dine under the stars.

Jane Restaurant's menu celebrates American bistro cuisine, focusing on fresh, locally sourced ingredients and simple yet flavorful preparations. The dishes are thoughtfully designed to appeal to a wide range of tastes, ensuring every guest finds something to enjoy. Signature dishes include the grilled artichoke appetizer, served with a tangy remoulade sauce, and the Jane Burger, a gourmet take on the classic burger that's become a favorite among regulars.

The menu also features a variety of salads, pasta dishes, and entrees, such as the seared salmon over a bed of quinoa salad, showcasing the kitchen's ability to blend health-conscious options with indulgent flavors.

Desserts at Jane Restaurant are not to be missed. A selection of housemade treats provides the perfect end to any meal. The wine list includes a thoughtful selection of local and international wines, complemented by craft beers and artisanal cocktails, ensuring that guests have the perfect pairing for their meal.

Jane Restaurant embodies the spirit of Santa Barbara dining at its best – where the food is made with care, the service is genuinely friendly, and the atmosphere is just right for any occasion. Whether you're celebrating a special event, enjoying a casual meal with family, or looking for a cozy spot for a romantic dinner, Jane Restaurant offers a dining experience that combines the best of Californian hospitality and culinary excellence.

Opal Restaurant and Bar

Opal Restaurant and Bar, located in the heart of downtown Santa Barbara, is a dynamic dining destination known for its eclectic California cuisine and vibrant atmosphere. Since its opening, Opal has become a favorite among locals and visitors alike, offering a culinary experience that blends global flavors with fresh, local ingredients. The restaurant's commitment to creating innovative dishes that are both delicious and visually stunning has earned it a loyal following and a place among Santa Barbara's top dining spots.

The ambiance of Opal Restaurant and Bar is inviting and lively. Its chic and colorful decor sets the stage for an unforgettable dining experience. The interior is adorned with contemporary art and warm lighting, creating a cozy yet sophisticated setting. With its energetic vibe and expertly crafted cocktails, the bar area is the perfect spot for a pre-dinner drink or a casual night out with friends.

Opal's menu is a testament to the creativity and passion of its culinary team, offering a range of dishes inspired by cuisines from around the world while staying rooted in the bounty of the Central Coast. Starters such as the lemon-grass crusted fresh salmon spring rolls and the spicy pecan-crusted goat cheese salad set the tone for a meal full of bold flavors and textures. Entrees like the pan-seared Chilean sea bass on a bed of lobster truffle risotto and the grilled filet mignon with gorgonzola butter showcase the kitchen's ability to elevate classic dishes with innovative twists.

In addition to its exceptional food, Opal Restaurant and Bar boasts an extensive wine list that highlights the best of Santa Barbara's vineyards and a selection of international wines. The cocktail menu is equally impressive, featuring original creations and classic drinks with a modern spin, all prepared with high-quality spirits and fresh ingredients.

Opal Restaurant and Bar is not just a place to eat; it's a destination for those seeking a lively dining atmosphere, exceptional food, and great company. Whether you're looking for a romantic dinner spot, a place to celebrate a special occasion, or a fun evening out, Opal offers an experience combining the best of California's culinary diversity and Santa Barbara's casual elegance.

Each of these establishments contributes to the rich culinary tapestry of Santa Barbara, offering unique dining experiences that cater to a wide range of tastes and preferences. Santa Barbara's dining scene promises memorable meals and flavors to savor, whether you're seeking the freshest seafood, the finest wines, or innovative plant-based cuisine.

4

Beyond Santa Barbara – Exploring the County

The Santa Ynez Valley: Wineries, Horseback Riding, and Danish Charm in Solvang

The Santa Ynez Valley, nestled in the heart of Santa Barbara County, is a picturesque region known for its sprawling vineyards, equestrian culture, and the quaint Danish village of Solvang. This area offers a unique blend of natural beauty, culinary excellence, and cultural diversity, making it a must-visit destination for wine enthusiasts, outdoor adventurers, and anyone looking to experience the charm of California's Central Coast.

Wineries in the Santa Ynez Valley

The Valley's Mediterranean climate and fertile soil make it an ideal location for wine production, particularly known for its excellent Pinot Noir, Chardonnay, and Syrah. Here are ten notable wineries that showcase the region's viticultural diversity:

1. **Sunstone Vineyards & Winery:** Known for its beautiful stone villa setting and organic vineyards, Sunstone offers a taste of Provence in California.

2. **Gainey Vineyard:** A family-owned winery that combines traditional winemaking techniques with innovative practices, producing a wide range of varietals.
3. **Fess Parker Winery & Vineyard:** This winery pays homage to its founder, the late actor Fess Parker, and is known for its Rhône and Burgundy varietals.
4. **Firestone Vineyard:** One of the first estate wineries in the region, Firestone is renowned for its Bordeaux-style wines and picturesque setting.
5. **Foxen Vineyard & Winery:** With a focus on sustainable farming, Foxen offers a range of critically acclaimed wines, including Pinot Noir and Chenin Blanc.
6. **Rusack Vineyards:** A boutique winery with a focus on limited production wines, Rusack is nestled in the rolling hills of Ballard Canyon.
7. **Demetria Estate:** Offers biodynamically farmed Rhône varietals in a tranquil, appointment-only setting, providing an intimate tasting experience.
8. **Beckmen Vineyards:** Specializing in Rhône varietals, Beckmen Vineyards is known for its biodynamic practices and robust, flavorful wines.
9. **Stolpman Vineyards:** This family-owned winery focuses on sustainable and organic vineyard practices, producing exceptional Syrah, Roussanne, and Sangiovese.
10. **Roblar Winery & Vineyards:** Combines wine tasting with culinary experiences, set in a beautiful estate that reflects the rustic elegance of the Valley.

Dining in the Santa Ynez Valley

The culinary scene in the Valley is as diverse and rich as its wines, with an array of restaurants serving everything from traditional Danish pastries to gourmet farm-to-table cuisine.

S.Y. Kitchen

Nestled in the charming town of Santa Ynez, within the picturesque Santa

Ynez Valley, S.Y. Kitchen offers a delightful retreat for those seeking a modern Italian dining experience. This restaurant has quickly become a beloved destination for both locals and visitors, praised for its fresh, homemade Italian dishes, rustic yet elegant ambiance, and warm hospitality. S.Y. Kitchen's commitment to utilizing the freshest local ingredients and traditional Italian cooking techniques has earned it a distinguished place in California's culinary scene.

The ambiance of S.Y. Kitchen combines rustic charm with contemporary elegance. The interior is warmly lit and welcoming, featuring exposed brick walls, wooden beams, and a cozy fireplace that adds to the restaurant's intimate atmosphere. The outdoor courtyard, adorned with string lights and surrounded by lush greenery, provides a perfect setting for al fresco dining, evoking the feeling of a serene Italian garden.

At the heart of S.Y. Kitchen's menu is a selection of dishes highlighting Italian cuisine's simplicity and richness. The kitchen, led by talented chefs, produces a variety of hand-made pastas, wood-fired pizzas, and inventive entrees that change with the seasons to reflect the freshest ingredients available. Signature dishes may include the Pappardelle with wild boar ragù, Margherita pizza with house-made mozzarella, and Grilled Branzino with seasonal vegetables. Each dish is carefully prepared and presented with an eye for detail, ensuring a memorable dining experience.

The bar at S.Y. Kitchen is just as impressive as its culinary offerings, featuring a carefully curated list of Italian and local wines that perfectly complement the menu's flavors. In addition, the cocktail program showcases inventive drinks crafted with house-made syrups, fresh juices, and premium spirits, adding a modern twist to classic Italian cocktails.

S.Y. Kitchen is more than just a restaurant; it's a destination that captures the essence of Italian dining while embracing the bounty of California's Central Coast. Whether you're enjoying a casual dinner in the cozy dining room, sipping a glass of wine in the courtyard, or celebrating a special occasion with friends and family, S.Y. Kitchen offers an experience that combines the best of Italian cuisine and California's fresh, local produce. It's a place where every visit promises delicious food, exceptional service, and an atmosphere that feels both familiar and enchanting.

Trattoria Grappolo

Trattoria Grappolo, nestled in the scenic Santa Ynez Valley, is a vibrant slice of Italy in California, renowned for its authentic Italian cuisine, warm hospitality, and charming ambiance. This beloved trattoria has earned its place as a favorite among locals and visitors alike, offering a dining experience that feels like a joyful gathering at a family table in Italy. The restaurant's commitment to using fresh, high-quality ingredients, combined with its traditional cooking methods, ensures that each dish is bursting with flavor and authenticity.

The ambiance at Trattoria Grappolo is cozy and inviting, with a rustic Italian decor that includes terracotta tiles, exposed brick walls, and an open kitchen that fills the space with enticing aromas. The atmosphere is lively and bustling, reminiscent of a classic Italian trattoria, where the sound of laughter and conversation adds to the vibrant dining experience. Outdoor seating is available, allowing guests to enjoy their meals under the California sky, surrounded by the picturesque beauty of the valley.

The menu at Trattoria Grappolo is a testament to the simplicity and richness of Italian cuisine, featuring a wide array of dishes that cater to various tastes and preferences. Starters like the Bruschetta al Pomodoro and Carpaccio di Manzo pave the way for a culinary journey through Italy. Handmade pastas, such as the Gnocchi al Gorgonzola and Linguine ai Frutti di Mare, showcase the kitchen's dedication to traditional techniques and flavors. The pizza, baked to perfection in a wood-fired oven, offers a crispy and delicious testament to Italian staples, while main courses like the Osso Buco and Bistecca alla Fiorentina highlight the robust flavors of Italian meat dishes.

Complementing the exquisite food is an extensive wine list, carefully selected to include both Italian and local wines that enhance the flavors of the menu. The knowledgeable staff are always ready to recommend the perfect pairing, ensuring a complete and harmonious dining experience.

Trattoria Grappolo is more than just a meal; it's an escape to Italy, where the joys of food, wine, and good company are celebrated in every bite. Whether you're there for a casual dinner, a romantic evening, or a festive gathering with friends and family, Trattoria Grappolo offers a warm welcome and an unforgettable taste of Italy in the heart of California's wine country.

Mad & Vin at The Landsby

Mad & Vin, located within The Landsby, an elegant boutique hotel in the heart of Solvang, California, offers a unique and sophisticated dining experience that captures the essence of the Santa Ynez Valley's rich culinary culture. The name "Mad & Vin" translates to "Food & Wine" in Danish, paying homage to Solvang's Danish heritage while focusing on the abundance of local produce and wines from the surrounding region. This restaurant has quickly become a favorite among both locals and visitors, celebrated for its modern American cuisine with a twist, cozy yet chic ambiance, and impeccable service.

The interior of Mad & Vin reflects the contemporary Scandinavian design of The Landsby, featuring a warm and welcoming atmosphere with a minimalist aesthetic. Natural light fills the space, highlighting the sleek furnishings, earthy tones, and touches of Danish elegance. The outdoor dining area, set in a beautifully landscaped courtyard, provides a serene setting for enjoying meals under the California sky, making it a perfect spot for al fresco dining.

Mad & Vin's menu celebrates local flavors and ingredients, meticulously crafted to showcase the best of what the Santa Ynez Valley has to offer. The kitchen team, led by talented chefs, creates innovative and comforting dishes, ensuring there's something to delight every palate. Seasonal menus might feature starters such as the locally sourced beet salad with goat cheese and pistachios, and main courses like the seared salmon with a citrus herb quinoa salad, or the signature burger topped with aged cheddar and house-made pickles.

The wine list at Mad & Vin is thoughtfully curated to complement the culinary offerings, featuring an extensive selection of local Santa Ynez Valley wines alongside notable Californian and international bottles. The restaurant also offers a variety of craft beers and creative cocktails, making it an ideal destination for wine enthusiasts and those looking to explore the vibrant local wine scene.

Mad & Vin at The Landsby provides a refined dining experience and serves as a warm and inviting gathering place where guests can enjoy the convivial spirit of Solvang. Whether starting your day with a gourmet breakfast, pausing for a leisurely lunch, or settling in for a romantic dinner, Mad & Vin promises a memorable meal that celebrates the art of food and wine in the heart of California's Danish village.

Ballard Inn & Gathering Table

The Ballard Inn & Gathering Table, nestled in the quaint town of Ballard within the idyllic Santa Ynez Valley, offers an exceptional dining experience that perfectly captures the essence of California's wine country. This charming inn and restaurant is celebrated for its elegant cuisine, intimate ambiance, and unparalleled hospitality, making it a beloved destination for food enthusiasts and those seeking a serene getaway.

The ambiance at the Ballard Inn & Gathering Table is one of understated elegance and warmth. The dining room, with its cozy fireplace, soft lighting, and refined decor, creates an inviting atmosphere that encourages guests to relax and savor every moment. The attention to detail in the design, from the carefully selected artworks to the comfortable seating, reflects the inn's commitment to providing a memorable dining experience.

At the helm of the kitchen is a team of talented chefs who craft dishes that are as visually stunning as they are delicious. The menu is a testament to the bounty of the Santa Ynez Valley, featuring locally sourced ingredients that are thoughtfully prepared to highlight their natural flavors. The cuisine can be described as innovative American with global influences, offering a range of dishes that appeal to a variety of tastes and dietary preferences.

Signature dishes at the Gathering Table may include succulent seafood creations, expertly grilled meats, and inventive vegetarian options, each presented with artistic flair. The chefs' dedication to quality and creativity is evident in every bite, whether it's a perfectly cooked piece of fish, a tender cut of locally raised beef, or a vibrant, farm-fresh vegetable dish.

The wine list at the Ballard Inn & Gathering Table is carefully curated to complement the menu, featuring an impressive selection of local Santa Ynez Valley wines alongside notable picks from further afield. The knowledgeable staff are always on hand to provide recommendations, ensuring that guests find the perfect wine to pair with their meal.

The Ballard Inn & Gathering Table is not just a place to dine; it's an experience that encompasses the best of Santa Ynez Valley's culinary scene and the warm hospitality that the region is known for. Whether celebrating a special occasion, enjoying a romantic dinner, or simply indulging in a gourmet meal, guests are treated to an evening of exquisite food, fine wine, and a welcoming atmosphere that feels like home.

Solvang Restaurant

Solvang Restaurant, located in the heart of Solvang, California's charming Danish village, is a beloved dining destination known for its authentic Danish cuisine and cozy, welcoming atmosphere. This iconic eatery has served locals and visitors for generations, offering a taste of Denmark in the Santa Ynez Valley. Famous for its traditional Danish dishes and homey ambiance, Solvang Restaurant provides a unique culinary experience that transports guests to the streets of Copenhagen.

The interior of Solvang Restaurant evokes a quaint Danish cottage, with warm wood accents, decorative plates adorning the walls, and Danish folk motifs that add to the authentic Scandinavian feel. The restaurant's casual and friendly atmosphere makes it the perfect spot for family meals, casual dining, or a hearty breakfast to start the day. During the warmer months, outdoor seating is available, allowing guests to enjoy their meals while taking in the sights and sounds of Solvang's bustling streets.

A standout feature of Solvang Restaurant is its famous æbleskiver, a traditional Danish pancake ball served with raspberry jam and a dusting of powdered sugar. These delightful treats are a must-try for anyone visiting Solvang and a signature restaurant dish. The menu also includes a variety of other Danish favorites, such as smørrebrød (open-faced sandwiches), frikadeller (Danish meatballs), and medisterpølse (Danish sausage), all prepared with authentic recipes and ingredients.

In addition to traditional Danish fare, Solvang Restaurant offers a selection of American breakfast and lunch classics, ensuring there's something to satisfy every palate. From pancakes and omelets to burgers and salads, the menu is designed to cater to a wide range of tastes while highlighting Danish cuisine's unique flavors.

Solvang Restaurant is more than just a place to eat; it's a culinary institution that embodies the spirit of Solvang's Danish heritage. Whether you're stopping by for a plate of æbleskiver, enjoying a leisurely brunch, or indulging in a Danish feast, Solvang Restaurant offers a warm welcome and a memorable dining experience that celebrates the rich culture and cuisine of Denmark, right in the heart of California's wine country.

AJ Spurs

AJ Spurs, located in the quaint town of Buellton, within the larger Santa Ynez Valley, is a dining establishment that transports guests back to the Old West with its unique ambiance, hearty meals, and warm hospitality. This restaurant is celebrated for offering a traditional steakhouse experience reminiscent of the cowboy era. It is a favorite among locals and visitors looking to taste Americana and generous portions of classic steakhouse fare.

The ambiance of AJ Spurs is meticulously crafted to evoke the feel of a bygone era, with rustic decor, vintage artifacts, and memorabilia that adorn the walls and spaces. The dining rooms are designed to resemble an old Western saloon or lodge, complete with wooden beams, cowboy boots, and antlers, creating a nostalgic and immersive atmosphere. It's not uncommon for the sounds of classic country music to fill the air, adding to the authentic Old West experience.

At the heart of AJ Spurs' menu is a selection of expertly prepared steaks, ribs, and chops, each cooked to perfection and served with various classic sides. The restaurant prides itself on its generous portions, ensuring no guest leaves hungry. Favorites include the "Trail Camp" rib-eye, the "Tombstone" sirloin, and the "Vaquero" chop, all of which are seasoned and grilled to highlight the natural flavors of the meat. In addition to the beef offerings, the menu features other hearty dishes such as chicken, seafood, and a selection of appetizers like the loaded potato skins and the spicy buffalo wings.

AJ Spurs is not just about the food; it's about providing a dining experience steeped in tradition and nostalgia. The service is known for being exceptionally friendly and attentive, with staff going out of their way to ensure guests feel welcome and satisfied. The restaurant also offers a selection of wines and beers, focusing on local brews that complement the robust flavors of the menu.

Dining at AJ Spurs is like stepping into a different time and place, where the spirit of the Old West and the comfort of classic American cuisine come together in perfect harmony. Whether you're celebrating a special occasion, enjoying a family dinner, or simply indulging in a steakhouse meal, AJ Spurs offers an unforgettable experience that captures the essence of cowboy culture and the culinary traditions of the American steakhouse.

Los Olivos Wine Merchant & Café

Nestled in the heart of Santa Barbara wine country, Los Olivos Wine Merchant & Café has carved out a niche as a must-visit destination for wine enthusiasts and foodies alike. This beloved establishment combines a world-class wine shop with a farm-to-table café, offering guests an opportunity to explore an extensive selection of local and international wines while enjoying dishes crafted from the freshest ingredients sourced from the surrounding area, including their own organic farm.

The ambiance of Los Olivos Wine Merchant & Café is both inviting and sophisticated, blending rustic charm with contemporary elegance. The café's interior exudes a warm, welcoming atmosphere, with natural light streaming in through large windows, illuminating the wood and stone accents that adorn the space. The outdoor seating area offers a serene dining environment, perfect for savoring a meal under the California sun amidst the picturesque backdrop of Los Olivos.

At the heart of the café's menu is a passion for showcasing the rich bounty of the region through dishes that are both simple and flavorful. The kitchen team emphasizes seasonality and sustainability, resulting in a menu that changes with the seasons but consistently offers a variety of options for all palates. Popular dishes include the wood-fired pizzas, adorned with a rotation of seasonal toppings; the grilled salmon, served atop a bed of locally grown vegetables; and the signature burger, featuring grass-fed beef and artisanal cheese. Each dish is presented with an eye for detail, ensuring a dining experience that delights the senses.

The wine selection at Los Olivos Wine Merchant & Café is nothing short of impressive, with a focus on local producers from Santa Barbara County and beyond. The knowledgeable staff are on hand to guide guests through the extensive list, offering recommendations and insights that enhance the overall dining experience. The café also hosts regular wine tastings and winemaker dinners, providing an intimate look into the world of wine and the opportunity to learn directly from the experts.

Los Olivos Wine Merchant & Café is more than just a dining destination; it's an experience that encapsulates the essence of California's wine country. Whether you're stopping by for a leisurely lunch, indulging in a wine tasting, or picking up a bottle from the wine shop, this establishment promises a warm welcome and an unforgettable journey through the flavors of the region.

The Hitching Post II

The Hitching Post II, nestled in the heart of the Santa Ynez Valley in Buellton, California, is a renowned restaurant that has become synonymous with the finest Santa Maria-style barbecue. Gaining widespread fame from its feature in the acclaimed movie "Sideways," The Hitching Post II has been a staple of the local dining scene since its opening, drawing food enthusiasts from all over the world to experience its authentic wood-fired cuisine and warm, rustic ambiance.

This iconic establishment boasts a cozy and inviting atmosphere, with interiors that reflect the rich heritage of the West. The dining space, adorned with Western memorabilia and a charming fireplace, creates a comfortable environment where guests can enjoy a meal in a setting that feels both nostalgic and timeless. The outdoor seating area offers a more casual dining experience, allowing guests to bask in the picturesque beauty of the valley while indulging in their meal.

At the heart of The Hitching Post II's menu is the traditional Santa Maria-style barbecue, known for its simple yet exquisite preparation and flavor. The restaurant prides itself on using only the finest quality meats, which are grilled over an open flame of red oak wood—a method that imparts a distinctive smokiness and depth of flavor to each dish. Signature offerings include the perfectly grilled ribeye steak, the succulent rack of lamb, and the famously tender barbecue pork ribs, each served with classic accompaniments like grilled vegetables, baked potatoes, and the house-made salsa.

Beyond its barbecue offerings, The Hitching Post II features an array of starters, salads, and seafood dishes that showcase the bounty of the Central Coast. The restaurant's commitment to freshness and quality is evident in every dish, from the crisp, locally sourced salads to the expertly prepared grilled artichokes.

The Hitching Post II is also renowned for its exceptional selection of wines, with a particular focus on Pinot Noir. The restaurant's own label, Hartley Ostini Hitching Post Wines, is produced in collaboration with local winemakers and offers a range of varietals that perfectly complement the flavors of the menu. The knowledgeable staff are always ready to assist guests in selecting the ideal wine pairing, enhancing the dining experience with their expertise.

Dining at The Hitching Post II is more than just a meal—it's an immersive experience that captures the spirit of the Santa Ynez Valley and its culinary traditions. Whether you're a local resident, a wine enthusiast, or a traveler seeking an authentic taste of California's barbecue heritage, The Hitching Post II promises a memorable meal that combines exceptional cuisine, a warm atmosphere, and the stunning backdrop of one of California's most picturesque regions.

Industrial Eats

Industrial Eats, located in Buellton within the heart of the Santa Ynez Valley, is a celebrated eatery that has quickly become a cornerstone of the local culinary scene. Known for its commitment to sustainability, locally sourced ingredients, and a menu that effortlessly blends innovation with comfort food classics, Industrial Eats offers a dining experience that is both casual and profoundly satisfying.

The restaurant's ambiance is unique and inviting, with an industrial-chic décor that reflects its name. The space is open and airy, featuring high ceilings, communal tables, and an open kitchen that allows diners to watch as their meals are artfully prepared. The walls are adorned with butcher charts and local art, contributing to the eatery's vibrant and eclectic atmosphere. The casual setting encourages guests to relax and enjoy a communal dining experience, making it a favorite gathering spot for locals and visitors alike.

At the core of Industrial Eats is a menu that emphasizes the bounty of the Central Coast. The kitchen team, led by passionate chefs, crafts dishes that are both simple and extraordinary, showcasing the quality of the ingredients. The eatery is renowned for its wood-fired pizzas, which feature a variety of gourmet toppings ranging from classic combinations to more adventurous flavors. The menu also includes an array of sandwiches, salads, and small plates, such as the house-cured meats and locally sourced cheese boards, which are perfect for sharing.

Sustainability is a key focus at Industrial Eats, with the restaurant sourcing its ingredients from local farms, ranches, and fisheries. This commitment not only supports the local economy but also ensures that each dish served is of the highest freshness and quality. The ever-changing menu reflects seasonal availability, offering guests a new experience with each visit.

Industrial Eats also boasts an impressive selection of wines and craft beers, carefully chosen to complement the menu and highlight the region's diverse viticulture. The knowledgeable staff are happy to recommend pairings, enhancing the overall dining experience.

Industrial Eats is more than just a restaurant; it celebrates community, sustainability, and the art of good eating. Whether you're stopping by for a quick lunch, a leisurely dinner, or to pick up some gourmet ingredients from the eatery's market, Industrial Eats offers a warm welcome and an unforgettable taste of the Santa Ynez Valley's culinary riches.

Shopping in Solvang and the Surrounding Area

Solvang, the Danish village in the Santa Ynez Valley, along with nearby towns, offers a variety of shops ranging from traditional Danish souvenirs to boutique fashion and artisan goods.

1. **Solvang Antiques, located in the heart of Solvang, specializes in fine antique furniture, art, and jewelry from around the world.**
2. **The Copenhagen House:** Features Danish modern design and artworks, along with Scandinavian goods in a sleek, contemporary space.
3. **Ingeborg's Danish Chocolates:** A Solvang tradition since 1961, offering handmade chocolates and confections using traditional Danish techniques.
4. **Jule Hus:** Known for its Christmas decorations and Nordic gifts, Jule Hus is a holiday wonderland year-round.
5. **Los Olivos General Store:** Offers a curated selection of local goods, home decor, and artisan products in the charming town of Los Olivos.
6. **The Book Loft:** Solvang's independent bookstore provides a wide selection of titles, Scandinavian literature, and gifts.
7. **Rasmussen's:** a one-stop shop for Scandinavian gifts, kitchenware, and home decor, bringing a taste of Denmark to California.
8. **First Street Leather:** Located in Solvang, this boutique offers high-quality leather goods, including jackets, bags, and accessories.
9. **Wendy Foster is a boutique chain located in Los Olivos and Santa Ynez that features** designer clothing, jewelry, and accessories.
10. **Elverhøj Museum of History & Art Gift Shop:** Located in Solvang, this unique gift shop is part of the Elverhøj Museum, dedicated to preserving and presenting Solvang's history and Danish culture.

The Santa Ynez Valley, with its blend of winemaking excellence, outdoor adventures, and cultural charm, offers visitors an unforgettable experience. From sipping world-class wines and dining on gourmet cuisine to exploring the Danish heritage of Solvang and shopping for unique local goods, the Valley is a testament to the diverse beauty and richness of Santa Barbara

County.

Carpinteria: Beaches, Avocados, and Family-Friendly Activities

Carpinteria, nestled along the scenic coastline of Santa Barbara County, is a charming small town that embodies the quintessence of California's laid-back lifestyle. Renowned for its pristine beaches, the world's safest avocado groves, and a plethora of family-friendly activities, Carpinteria offers a serene escape from the hustle and bustle of city life. This idyllic town provides a unique blend of natural beauty, agricultural heritage, and recreational activities, making it a perfect destination for families, nature lovers, and anyone looking to unwind in a picturesque setting.

Pristine Beaches

- **Carpinteria State Beach:** Often referred to as the "world's safest beach," Carpinteria State Beach boasts gentle waves, making it ideal for swimming, sunbathing, and family outings. The beach is also a popular spot for camping, with well-equipped facilities that allow visitors to fall asleep to the sound of the ocean.
- **Rincon Point:** Known as one of the premier surfing spots in California, Rincon Point offers excellent conditions for surfers of all levels. While the waves attract surf enthusiasts, the beach's beauty and tranquility make it a delightful spot for spectators and families to relax and enjoy the coastal ambiance.

Avocado Capital

Carpinteria proudly holds the title of "Avocado Capital of the World," and its agricultural landscapes are dotted with lush avocado orchards. The town celebrates its avocado heritage annually with the Carpinteria Avocado Festival, a family-friendly event that features avocado-themed foods, crafts, and entertainment. This festival is a testament to the community's pride in its agricultural roots and offers visitors a taste of local flavors and traditions.

Family-Friendly Activities

- **Tar Pits Park:** An intriguing natural site, the Carpinteria Tar Pits Park is one of the few places in the world where natural asphalt seeps up through the ground. Families can explore the park's trails, view the tar pits, and learn about the area's prehistoric significance.
- **Tomol Interpretive Play Area:** Inspired by the Chumash Native American culture, this unique playground in Carpinteria State Beach offers children a fun and educational experience. The play area features a replica Tomol (a traditional plank canoe), providing kids with an imaginative and interactive way to learn about the region's indigenous history.
- **Carpinteria Salt Marsh Nature Park:** A haven for bird watchers and nature enthusiasts, this protected wetland offers guided tours and self-guided walks. Visitors can observe a diverse array of bird species, plants, and wildlife, highlighting the importance of coastal ecosystems.
- **Alpaca Farm Tours:** Just outside Carpinteria, several alpaca farms offer tours where families can get up close and personal with these gentle animals. It's a unique opportunity to learn about alpaca care, wool production, and sustainable farming practices.
- **Linden Avenue:** The heart of Carpinteria's downtown area, Linden Avenue, is lined with quaint shops, cafes, and restaurants. Families can enjoy a leisurely stroll, shop for local crafts and produce, or dine at one of the many eateries offering everything from casual bites to gourmet cuisine.

Carpinteria's blend of natural beauty, cultural richness, and family-oriented activities makes it a jewel along the California coast. Whether you're looking to catch a wave at Rincon Point, indulge in the local avocado culture, or simply enjoy a day under the sun at Carpinteria State Beach, this charming town offers a peaceful yet vibrant setting for visitors of all ages.

Montecito: Luxury, Gardens, and Celebrity Sightings with Exquisite Dining

Montecito, nestled between the majestic Santa Ynez Mountains and the crystal-clear waters of the Pacific Ocean, epitomizes luxury living on California's Central Coast. This exclusive community, known for its stunning estates, lush gardens, and as a haven for celebrities, offers an unparalleled blend of natural beauty and opulence. Beyond the grandiose, Montecito also boasts some of the finest dining experiences, where exquisite cuisine meets impeccable service in settings ranging from the elegantly casual to the distinctly sophisticated.

The Essence of Montecito

Montecito's charm lies in its ability to blend privacy and luxury seamlessly. The area's well-manicured public spaces and private estates are home to some of the most exquisite gardens in California, including the historic Lotusland, a spectacular 37-acre estate filled with rare and exotic plants. The serene environment, coupled with Montecito's temperate climate, makes it a year-round paradise for those seeking tranquility and beauty.

Celebrity sightings are common, with many A-listers calling Montecito their home or their favorite getaway spot. However, the community maintains a respectful atmosphere, where privacy is cherished and the star-studded presence adds to the locale's allure rather than overshadowing it.

Dining in Montecito

Montecito's dining scene reflects its overall ethos, offering a variety of culinary experiences that cater to sophisticated palates. Here are 10 restaurants that stand out for their exceptional cuisine, ambiance, and service:

The Stonehouse at San Ysidro Ranch

Nestled within the lush, tranquil grounds of the historic San Ysidro Ranch in Montecito, The Stonehouse stands as a pinnacle of fine dining, offering an exquisite culinary experience that marries rustic elegance with unparalleled natural beauty. This esteemed restaurant, located in a 19th-century citrus packing house, has been meticulously restored to reflect the rich heritage of its surroundings, providing guests with a dining atmosphere that is both sophisticated and warmly inviting.

Surrounded by the ranch's vibrant gardens and overlooking the Pacific Ocean, The Stonehouse offers a truly unmatched ambiance. The dining room, with its original stone fireplace and rich wooden beams, exudes an old-world charm complemented by the restaurant's outdoor terrace. Here, guests can dine under the canopy of stars amidst the gentle flicker of lanterns and the soothing sounds of a nearby creek, making every meal memorable.

The cuisine at The Stonehouse reflects California's bountiful produce and the culinary team's commitment to farm-to-table principles. Utilizing the freshest ingredients, many of which are sourced directly from the ranch's own organic gardens, the menu offers a sophisticated blend of contemporary American dishes with Mediterranean influences. Each creation is thoughtfully prepared and beautifully presented, showcasing the flavors and textures of the ingredients in their purest form.

Signature dishes may include the likes of grilled prime beef filet with truffled potato puree, dayboat scallops with cauliflower and golden raisins, or stone oven-baked flatbreads adorned with seasonal toppings. The menu is complemented by an extensive wine list highlighting the finest selections from local Santa Barbara County vineyards and international treasures, ensuring a perfect pairing for every dish.

The Stonehouse at San Ysidro Ranch is more than just a restaurant; it is an experience that captivates all the senses. From the enchanting setting and the impeccable service to the exquisite cuisine and fine wines, dining here is a celebration of the best California's culinary scene has to offer. It is a destination where special occasions are marked, milestones are celebrated, and every visit feels like a retreat into a world of beauty, elegance, and gastronomic delight.

Lucky's

Lucky's, located in the affluent and picturesque town of Montecito, California, stands as a beacon of classic steakhouse tradition, blending impeccable service with a sophisticated yet unpretentious ambiance. Esteemed for its prime cuts of beef, fresh seafood, and comprehensive wine list, Lucky's has earned a reputation not just as a dining establishment but as a cherished institution within the Montecito community and beyond. Its fame is bolstered by frequent visits from celebrities and locals alike, drawn by the restaurant's commitment to quality and its classic, timeless charm.

Upon entering Lucky's, guests are enveloped in an atmosphere that harks back to the golden age of steakhouses. The interior exudes elegance and comfort, featuring rich wood paneling, intimate lighting, and classic décor, including vintage photographs and plush seating. Whether opting to dine in the cozy, inviting dining room or preferring the bar's lively atmosphere, Lucky's offers an environment where every meal feels like a special occasion.

At the heart of Lucky's menu is a selection of exceptional steaks. Sourced from the finest producers and grilled to perfection, options range from the tender filet mignon to the robust bone-in ribeye, each served with a choice of classic steakhouse sides like creamed spinach, sautéed mushrooms, and hand-cut French fries. Beyond steaks, the menu features a variety of seafood dishes, including freshly shucked oysters, chilled lobster, and a daily selection of fish, ensuring there's something to satisfy every palate.

The wine list at Lucky's is meticulously curated, offering an impressive selection of local Santa Barbara wines alongside renowned labels from around the world, designed to complement the rich flavors of the menu. The cocktail program, too, is notable, featuring a mix of classic drinks and house specialties, all crafted with premium spirits and the freshest ingredients.

Dining at Lucky's is more than just enjoying a meal; it's an experience that celebrates the art of fine dining in an elegant and relaxed setting. Whether it's a casual dinner, a special celebration, or a night out enjoying cocktails and the company of friends, Lucky's provides a backdrop of unmatched sophistication and warmth. In a world where dining trends come and go, Lucky's remains a steadfast favorite, offering a timeless dining experience that is both memorable and distinctly Montecito.

The Honor Bar

Nestled in the heart of Montecito, California, The Honor Bar is a vibrant and cozy spot known for its exceptional food, inviting atmosphere, and meticulous attention to quality. A part of the Hillstone Restaurant Group, The Honor Bar is celebrated for creating a dining experience that is both sophisticated and relaxed, making it a favored destination for both locals and visitors seeking a casual yet refined eating and drinking experience.

The ambiance of The Honor Bar is chic and intimate, with a design that marries modern elegance with comfort. The interior features rich wood finishes, contemporary art pieces, and plush seating encouraging diners to linger and enjoy. Large windows allow natural light to fill the space, creating a warm and welcoming environment. The outdoor patio offers an idyllic setting for al fresco dining, where guests can enjoy the beautiful Montecito weather amidst lush greenery.

At the core of The Honor Bar's menu is a selection of meticulously crafted dishes that emphasize freshness and flavor. The restaurant is renowned for its sandwiches, including the crispy chicken sandwich and the French dip, each made with high-quality ingredients and served with house-made sides. The menu also features a variety of salads, like the kale and rotisserie chicken salad, which are hearty and flavorful. Small plates, such as the deviled eggs and sushi-grade tuna tartare, are perfect for sharing and pair excellently with the restaurant's drink offerings.

The Honor Bar's drink menu is as thoughtfully curated as its food offerings, featuring a range of craft cocktails, premium wines, and artisanal beers. The cocktail program showcases classic drinks with a modern twist, made with top-shelf spirits and fresh, high-quality mixers. The wine list highlights selections from local vineyards and international favorites, ensuring the perfect pairing for any meal.

Service at The Honor Bar is attentive and warm, with a staff committed to providing an exceptional dining experience. From the bartenders crafting perfect cocktails to the servers offering recommendations and ensuring every detail is attended to, the team at The Honor Bar makes each visit memorable.

The Honor Bar is more than just a restaurant; it's a gathering place where the simple joys of good food, drinks, and company are celebrated. Whether stopping by for a drink and a snack or settling in for a full meal, guests at The Honor Bar can expect a welcoming atmosphere, exceptional service, and a dining experience that captures the casual elegance of Montecito.

Tre Lune

Tre Lune, nestled in the charming and upscale community of Montecito, California, is an exquisite Italian restaurant that captures the essence of Italy's rich culinary tradition. Celebrated for its authentic cuisine, elegant ambiance, and warm hospitality, Tre Lune has become a beloved destination for both locals and visitors seeking an exceptional Italian dining experience.

Upon entering Tre Lune, guests are greeted by a cozy and sophisticated atmosphere that feels both welcoming and refined. The decor pays homage to classic Italian aesthetics, featuring warm hues, intimate lighting, and tasteful artwork that together create a perfect backdrop for a memorable meal. The dining space is designed to evoke the comfort and familiarity of a traditional Italian trattoria, while still maintaining a sense of upscale Montecito charm.

The menu at Tre Lune is a testament to the simplicity and richness of Italian cuisine, focusing on high-quality ingredients and time-honored recipes. Dishes are prepared with meticulous care and a passion for showcasing the authentic flavors of Italy. From handmade pastas and fresh seafood to expertly grilled meats and artisanal pizzas, each menu item is a celebration of culinary craftsmanship.

Signature dishes include the Spaghetti al Pomodoro, featuring perfectly cooked pasta tossed in a vibrant tomato sauce with fresh basil; the Risotto ai Frutti di Mare, a rich and creamy risotto adorned with an abundance of seafood; and the Vitello Milanese, a tender veal chop breaded and fried to golden perfection, served with arugula and cherry tomatoes. The menu also offers a selection of antipasti, insalate, and contorni to complement the main courses, ensuring a complete and harmonious meal.

The wine list at Tre Lune is carefully curated to pair beautifully with the menu, featuring an extensive selection of Italian wines from various regions, as well as choices from local California vineyards. Whether you prefer a robust red, a crisp white, or a sparkling Prosecco, Tre Lune's knowledgeable staff are ready to assist you in finding the perfect wine to enhance your dining experience.

Dining at Tre Lune is not just about enjoying great food; it's about immersing oneself in an atmosphere that celebrates the joys of Italian culture, cuisine, and camaraderie. Whether you're gathering for a family meal, a romantic dinner, or a festive occasion with friends, Tre Lune offers an unforgettable experience that brings a taste of Italy to the heart of Montecito.

Cava Restaurant & Bar

Cava Restaurant & Bar, nestled in the charming coastal village of Montecito, California, offers a vibrant fusion of Latin American, Spanish, and Mediterranean cuisines in an atmosphere that's as warm and lively as the dishes it serves. This beloved dining spot draws inspiration from the rich culinary traditions of these regions, presenting a menu that is both diverse and flavorful, set against a backdrop of colorful, eclectic decor that captures the spirit of a festive hacienda.

Upon entering Cava, guests are greeted by a setting combining rustic charm and a touch of elegance. The interior is adorned with bright, Mediterranean-inspired colors, terracotta tiles, and an array of Latin American and Spanish art and artifacts, creating an inviting and visually stimulating space. The outdoor patio, a hidden gem, offers an enchanting dining experience under the stars, surrounded by lush foliage and the gentle murmur of a nearby fountain, making it an ideal spot for al fresco dining.

The menu at Cava Restaurant & Bar is a testament to the creativity and passion of its culinary team. It features a wide range of tapas, perfect for sharing and exploring the variety of flavors. Dishes such as ceviche, made with the freshest seafood, empanadas filled with savory ingredients, and patatas bravas, a Spanish classic, are just a few examples of the appetizers that tantalize the taste buds. The entrees are equally impressive, with highlights including the paella, rich with saffron and brimming with seafood and chorizo, and the churrasco, a perfectly grilled steak accompanied by chimichurri sauce.

Cava's dedication to authentic flavors extends to its drink menu, which boasts an impressive selection of wines from Spain and South America alongside signature cocktails incorporating fresh fruits, herbs, and premium spirits. The sangria, a house specialty, is a must-try, perfectly balancing sweetness and zest, and is available by the glass or pitcher.

Service at Cava is attentive and friendly. The team is eager to share their knowledge of the menu and help guests navigate the wide array of culinary delights. The staff's passion for the cuisine and culture of Latin America and the Mediterranean is evident, enhancing the dining experience with their enthusiasm and expertise.

Cava Restaurant & Bar is more than just a meal; it celebrates vibrant flavors, a lively atmosphere, and the joy of sharing good food with good company. Whether you're in the mood for a romantic dinner, a festive gathering with friends, or simply a night out enjoying exquisite cuisine in a beautiful setting, Cava promises an unforgettable dining experience that transports you to the sunny shores of the Mediterranean and the vibrant streets of Latin America.

Via Vai Trattoria & Pizzeria

Nestled in the picturesque community of Montecito, California, Via Vai Trattoria & Pizzeria stands as a beloved emblem of authentic Italian cuisine, offering a slice of Italy in the heart of California's wine country. This charming eatery is celebrated for its traditional Italian dishes, wood-fired pizzas, and a warm, inviting atmosphere that makes every diner feel like part of the family. With its dedication to authenticity and quality, Via Vai has garnered a loyal following among locals and visitors alike, eager to indulge in the rich flavors and rustic charm of genuine Italian dining.

Upon entering Via Vai, guests are immediately enveloped in a cozy and welcoming ambiance that pays homage to classic Italian trattorias. The interior exudes a rustic elegance, with exposed wood beams, terracotta tiles, and walls adorned with Italian art and photographs that capture the spirit of Italy's diverse regions. The outdoor patio offers a delightful al fresco dining experience, where guests can enjoy the beautiful Montecito weather while surrounded by lush greenery and the gentle murmur of conversation.

At the heart of Via Vai's menu is a passion for the traditional flavors of Italy, expertly crafted by a team of skilled chefs using the freshest ingredients. The restaurant takes pride in its selection of wood-fired pizzas, each made with hand-tossed dough, San Marzano tomatoes, and the finest mozzarella, then baked to perfection in a classic Italian oven. Signature pizzas include the Margherita, with its simple yet sublime combination of flavors, and the Quattro Stagioni, a delightful representation of the four seasons.

Beyond pizza, Via Vai offers a wide range of Italian favorites, from freshly made pasta dishes like the indulgent Fettuccine al Tartufo to hearty entrees such as the Bistecca Fiorentina, a Tuscan-style steak grilled to succulent perfection. The menu also features an array of antipasti, insalate, and dolci, each dish thoughtfully prepared to transport diners on a culinary journey through Italy.

The beverage selection at Via Vai complements the menu beautifully, featuring a curated list of Italian wines, from robust Chiantis to crisp Pinot Grigios, alongside local California wines that reflect the region's viticultural excellence. The restaurant also offers a variety of Italian aperitifs, digestifs, and crafted cocktails, perfect for starting or finishing your meal on a high note.

Via Vai Trattoria & Pizzeria is more than just a restaurant; it celebrates Italian culinary traditions, family, and the simple joys of sharing a meal. Whether you're in the mood for a casual pizza night, a romantic dinner, or a special celebration with loved ones, Via Vai promises an authentic Italian dining experience that's rich in flavor and steeped in tradition, all within the beautiful setting of Montecito.

Oliver's of Montecito

Oliver's of Montecito is a premier dining destination for its commitment to gourmet plant-based cuisine. It offers a sophisticated and innovative menu in one of California's most luxurious neighborhoods. This upscale restaurant is renowned for its exquisite vegan dishes, elegant ambiance, and exceptional service, making it a favorite among health-conscious diners and food enthusiasts alike. Oliver's has successfully challenged the conventions of plant-based dining, presenting dishes that are as delicious and satisfying as they are healthful and sustainable.

The ambiance at Oliver's of Montecito is refined and inviting, blending contemporary design with natural elements to create a serene dining environment. The interior is beautifully decorated with a minimalist aesthetic, featuring clean lines, lush greenery, and soft, ambient lighting that together create a stylish and comfortable space. The outdoor patio offers an idyllic setting for al fresco dining, where guests can enjoy the mild Montecito climate amidst beautifully landscaped surroundings.

At the heart of Oliver's menu is an array of creatively crafted dishes showcasing plant-based ingredients' versatility and depth. Each dish is thoughtfully prepared to highlight natural flavors and textures, from starters and salads to main courses and desserts. Signature dishes include the Truffle Mushroom Pizza, made with a rich cashew cream and topped with wild mushrooms and truffle oil, and the Jackfruit Tacos, which feature marinated jackfruit and a vibrant array of fresh toppings. The restaurant also offers an impressive selection of raw dishes, innovative sides, and decadent desserts that defy the typical expectations of vegan cuisine.

The beverage program at Oliver's is equally impressive. It features organic and biodynamic wines from around the world, craft cocktails made with fresh juices and premium spirits, and a selection of non-alcoholic options that are as inventive as they are refreshing. Each drink is carefully selected or crafted to complement the menu's flavors, enhancing the dining experience.

Service at Oliver's of Montecito is attentive and knowledgeable, with a staff that takes pride in the restaurant's culinary offerings and is eager to assist guests in navigating the menu. Whether you're a long-time vegan, exploring plant-based eating for the first time, or simply searching for a nourishing and indulgent meal, Oliver's provides a dining experience that is sure to impress.

Oliver's of Montecito is more than just a restaurant; it celebrates plant-based cuisine at its finest, set against one of California's most enchanting locales. With its commitment to quality, innovation, and sustainability,

Oliver's offers a memorable dining experience and a testament to the possibilities of gourmet vegan cuisine.

Bettina

Bettina, nestled in the charming Montecito Country Mart, has quickly become a beloved staple in the Santa Barbara dining scene, celebrated for its artisanal, wood-fired pizzas and warm, inviting atmosphere. This cozy pizzeria blends the casual spirit of California with the traditional techniques and flavors of Neapolitan pizza making, creating a dining experience that's both authentic and uniquely local.

The ambiance at Bettina is relaxed and welcoming. Its modern design pays homage to the classic pizzeria while infusing it with a contemporary flair. The space features an open kitchen, allowing diners to watch as their pizzas are expertly crafted and baked to perfection in the wood-fired oven. With its stylish yet unpretentious decor, Bettina provides the perfect backdrop for a casual lunch, a family dinner, or a night out with friends.

At the heart of Bettina's menu is a selection of pizzas that stand out for their exquisite, charred crusts and high-quality, locally sourced toppings. From the classic Margherita, with its simple yet sublime combination of San Marzano tomatoes, mozzarella, basil, and extra virgin olive oil, to more inventive offerings like the pizza with house-made sausage, kale, and pickled peppers, each pizza is a testament to the art of pizza making. Beyond pizzas, Bettina offers a variety of antipasti, salads, and small plates, such as marinated olives and wood-roasted vegetables, that showcase the bounty of the Central Coast.

The drink menu at Bettina is thoughtfully curated to complement the flavors of the food, featuring a selection of local wines, craft beers, and artisanal cocktails. Whether you're in the mood for a refreshing spritz, a glass of natural wine, or a crisp lager, you'll find the perfect accompaniment to your meal.

Bettina is not just a pizzeria; it's a gathering place where the joys of shared meals and good conversation are celebrated. The friendly staff, the delicious, thoughtfully prepared food, and the cozy, inviting atmosphere make Bettina a must-visit destination for anyone looking to enjoy some of the best pizza Santa Barbara has to offer, all in the beautiful setting of Montecito.

Each dining destination in Montecito contributes to the area's reputation as a haven for those who appreciate the finer things in life, offering experiences that range from the casual and cozy to the refined and luxurious. Whether you're in the mood for an Italian feast, a plant-based gourmet meal, or a classic steak dinner, Montecito's dining scene promises an unforgettable culinary journey.

The Channel Islands: An Adventurer's Guide to the "Galápagos of North America"

The Channel Islands, often called the "Galápagos of North America," are a unique archipelago off the coast of Southern California. This guide aims to delve into the wonders of these islands, providing adventurers with all they need to explore this remarkable and relatively untouched natural sanctuary. Comprising five main islands — Anacapa, Santa Cruz, Santa Rosa, San Miguel, and Santa Barbara — each island offers distinct experiences, landscapes, and wildlife, making the Channel Islands a must-visit destination for nature enthusiasts, hikers, kayakers, and anyone with a love for the outdoors.

Getting There

Island Packers provides access to the Channel Islands primarily through boat services, operating out of Ventura and Oxnard or by plane for certain destinations. Planning your trip in advance is crucial, as access can be affected by weather conditions and visitor limits to protect the islands' delicate ecosystems.

What to Explore

Anacapa Island: The closest island to the mainland, Anacapa is famous for its iconic Arch Rock, a massive 40-foot natural arch. Anacapa's cliffside trails offer breathtaking ocean views and a chance to see the island's large seabird colonies, including the western gull and the rare Scripps's murrelet.

Santa Cruz Island: The largest of the Channel Islands, Santa Cruz is a hiker's paradise with over 250 species of plants and 60 species of birds. The island's diverse landscapes include rugged coastline, scenic beaches, and the Painted Cave, one of the world's largest sea caves. Activities include hiking, camping, kayaking, and snorkeling.

Santa Rosa Island: Santa Rosa features diverse landscapes, from its stunning beaches like Water Canyon Beach to the historic Vail and Vickers ranch. The island is also home to the unique Torrey Pines, the rarest pine species in the United States.

San Miguel Island: The westernmost island, San Miguel, is known for its vast pinniped colonies. Point Bennett hosts one of the world's largest gatherings of seals and sea lions. The island's history as a military outpost adds an intriguing layer to its natural beauty.

Santa Barbara Island: The smallest island, Santa Barbara, is known for its seabird colonies and excellent opportunities for diving and snorkeling in its kelp forests.

What to Do

- **Hiking:** Each island offers a variety of trails, ranging from easy walks to challenging hikes, showcasing the islands' unique geography and biodiversity.
- **Camping:** Limited camping facilities are available on the islands, providing a unique way to experience their natural beauty up close. Reservations are a must.
- **Kayaking:** The Channel Islands' rugged coastline and sea caves offer some of the best kayaking experiences in California. Guided tours are available.
- **Wildlife Watching:** From endemic island foxes to marine life, such as dolphins and whales, the islands offer incredible wildlife-watching opportunities.
- **Snorkeling and Diving:** The islands' clear waters and rich marine life make for excellent snorkeling and diving.

Tips for Visitors

- **Prepare for Isolation:** The islands offer limited facilities; visitors must bring all necessary supplies, including water and food.
- **Respect the Environment:** The fragile ecosystems of the Channel Islands require visitors to practice Leave No Trace principles to preserve their natural beauty.
- **Check Weather and Conditions:** Weather can change rapidly, and sea conditions can affect boat crossings. Always check the forecast and plan accordingly.
- **Educate Yourself:** The islands have a rich history and unique ecosystems. Learning about them before your visit can enhance your experience.

The Channel Islands National Park is a rare opportunity to explore untouched wilderness and experience the diversity of California's natural beauty. Whether you're an avid hiker, wildlife enthusiast, or simply seeking solitude in nature, the Channel Islands offer an unparalleled adventure.

5

Activities and Experiences

Outdoor Adventures in Santa Barbara: Hiking, Surfing, and Kayaking

Santa Barbara, known for its stunning coastal landscapes and mountainous backdrop, is a haven for outdoor enthusiasts. The region offers a plethora of activities ranging from serene hikes and thrilling surf breaks to peaceful kayaking journeys along the coastline or through gentle rivers. Here's a guide to some of the best spots in Santa Barbara for hiking, surfing, and kayaking, ensuring an unforgettable outdoor adventure.

Hiking

Santa Barbara's diverse terrain offers numerous hiking trails that cater to all levels of experience, each providing unique vistas and experiences:

- **Inspiration Point:** This accessible yet rewarding hike offers panoramic views of Santa Barbara, the ocean, and the Channel Islands. The trailhead starts at Tunnel Road, leading to a moderately challenging path that culminates in breathtaking views.
- **Rattlesnake Canyon Trail:** Ideal for nature lovers, this trail meanders through a lush canyon with a creek, offering a shady path and the opportunity to spot local wildlife.

- **Gaviota Peak Trail:** A more challenging hike, this trail offers stunning views from the highest point in the Gaviota State Park. The effort is rewarded with panoramic vistas of the coast and the possibility of a dip in the natural hot springs near the trail's end.
- **Seven Falls Trail:** A favorite among locals, this trail features a series of waterfalls and swimming holes, especially vibrant after rainfall. It's a moderate hike with some rocky terrain, located in the front country of the Santa Ynez Mountains.
- **Montecito Peak:** For a more strenuous hike, Montecito Peak provides a challenging ascent with rewarding panoramic views at the summit. The trail starts from the Cold Springs trailhead and winds through lush chaparral and oak woodlands.
- **Douglas Family Preserve:** For a leisurely walk with ocean views, this off-leash dog-friendly park offers easy trails along the cliffs overlooking Arroyo Burro Beach, perfect for families and casual hikers.

Surfing

Santa Barbara's coastline is renowned for its surf spots, catering to all skill levels, from beginners to seasoned surfers:

- **Rincon Point:** Known as the "Queen of the Coast," Rincon Point is one of the best surf spots in California. Its world-class waves make it a popular destination for surfers worldwide.
- **Leadbetter Beach:** Perfect for beginners and longboarders, it offers gentle, rolling waves and a laid-back atmosphere, ideal for those looking to catch their first wave or enjoy a relaxed surf session.
- **Jalama Beach:** A bit of a drive from Santa Barbara, Jalama Beach is known for its powerful waves and less crowded conditions, suitable for more experienced surfers.
- **Mondos Beach:** Ideal for beginners, Mondos offers gentle, long-rolling waves. Schools like the Santa Barbara Surf School offer lessons here, providing a safe and encouraging environment for new surfers.

- **Carpinteria State Beach:** This is another great spot for novice surfers, with mild waves and a sandy bottom. Due to the forgiving conditions, surf schools frequently conduct lessons here.
- **Santa Claus Lane Beach:** Popular for its consistent surf, this spot caters to intermediate surfers but is also manageable for beginners. Local surf shops like the Carpinteria Surf Company offer rentals and lessons.

Kayaking

Kayaking in Santa Barbara provides a unique perspective of the area's stunning natural beauty, with options for sea or lake paddling:

- **Channel Islands National Park:** Kayaking around the Channel Islands offers a spectacular experience. You can explore sea caves and kelp forests and encounter marine wildlife. Guided tours are available, providing safe and informative adventures.
- **Santa Barbara Harbor:** For a more urban kayaking experience, the Santa Barbara Harbor and shoreline offer calm waters and scenic views of the city and mountains. It's perfect for a leisurely paddle and accessible to kayakers of all levels.
- **Lake Cachuma:** Nestled in the Santa Ynez Valley, Lake Cachuma offers freshwater kayaking with opportunities to observe local birdlife and enjoy the tranquil natural surroundings away from the coastal winds.
- **El Capitán State Beach:** For ocean kayaking with a chance to land on a secluded beach, head to El Capitán. Aquasports has a kayak kiosk right on the beach during the summer months, making rentals convenient.

Preparation and Safety

When embarking on outdoor adventures in Santa Barbara, it's crucial to prepare adequately:

- Check weather and tide conditions before heading out, especially for surfing and kayaking.

- Ensure you have the proper gear, including safety equipment, and understand the area's regulations and access points.
- Stay hydrated and protected from the sun, and always respect the natural environment to preserve its beauty and wildlife.

Santa Barbara's diverse landscapes offer a playground for outdoor enthusiasts, whether you're looking to hike the rugged trails, surf the dynamic waves, or paddle along the serene waters. With careful planning and respect for nature, these activities can provide an exhilarating and fulfilling way to experience the area's natural wonders.

Cultural Experiences in Santa Barbara: Museums, Galleries, and Theaters

Santa Barbara's cultural landscape is a vibrant tapestry of history, art, and performance, offering a plethora of experiences for those seeking to immerse themselves in the city's rich heritage and dynamic art scene. Santa Barbara caters to a diverse array of interests and tastes, from historic museums and avant-garde galleries to iconic theaters and educational centers.

Museums

- **Santa Barbara Museum of Art (SBMA):** Situated in the city's downtown, SBMA houses an extensive collection of artworks spanning across continents and centuries, with notable strengths in American, Asian, and European art.
- **Santa Barbara Historical Museum:** This museum delves into the local history, offering exhibits that cover the region's development from the Chumash civilization to modern times, enriched with artifacts, photographs, and documents.
- **Santa Barbara Maritime Museum:** Celebrating the maritime heritage of the region, this museum offers exhibits on naval history, oceanography, and marine conservation, featuring interactive displays and historic

artifacts.
- **MOXI, The Wolf Museum of Exploration + Innovation:** A hub for interactive science and creativity, MOXI engages visitors with exhibits in technology, engineering, arts, and math, making it ideal for families and curious minds.
- **Reagan Ranch Center:** This museum provides insight into Ronald Reagan's life and presidency and showcases the history and legacy of his time in office, with a special focus on his ranch in the Santa Ynez Mountains.
- **Santa Barbara Carriage Museum:** This unique museum displays a collection of horse-drawn carriages, wagons, and historical memorabilia, offering a glimpse into the transportation methods of the past.
- **Santa Barbara Museum of Natural History:** Located near Mission Santa Barbara, this museum offers exhibits on regional natural history, including ocean life, bird habitats, and indigenous cultures, set in a charming creek-side setting with nature trails and a planetarium, making it a captivating educational experience for all ages.

Galleries

- **Sullivan Goss - An American Gallery:** Specializing in American art, Sullivan Goss offers diverse historical and contemporary works, providing insight into the country's artistic evolution.
- **Gallery 113:** Run by the Santa Barbara Art Association, this gallery features a wide range of artworks by local artists, offering a taste of the region's vibrant art community.
- **10 West Gallery:** Focused on contemporary art, 10 West Gallery showcases innovative works by local and regional artists, presenting cutting-edge exhibitions in various mediums.

Theaters

- **The Granada Theatre:** A historical landmark and the city's premier

venue for performing arts, The Granada Theatre hosts a variety of performances, from classical concerts to modern theatrical productions.
- **The Lobero Theatre:** California's oldest continuously operating theater, the Lobero offers an intimate setting for a wide range of performances, including jazz concerts, dance recitals, and plays.
- **Ensemble Theatre Company at The New Vic:** Known for its high-quality productions of contemporary and classic plays, this theater company provides compelling theatrical experiences in a state-of-the-art venue.
- **The Arlington Theatre:** An architectural gem in Santa Barbara, The Arlington Theatre is not only a movie palace but also a venue for concerts, lectures, and performances, known for its Spanish Colonial Revival style and ornate interior.

Cultural Immersion

To fully experience the cultural vibrancy of Santa Barbara:

- Participate in the city's numerous arts festivals, which showcase local and international talent in various forms, from film and music to visual arts and dance.
- Explore the Funk Zone, an area known for its dynamic art scene. Its galleries, studios, and murals reflect the city's contemporary artistic pulse.
- Engage with First Thursday events, where downtown Santa Barbara comes alive with cultural activities, open galleries, and live performances, offering a festive atmosphere to celebrate the arts.

Santa Barbara's cultural scene is a rich mosaic of history, art, and entertainment, providing endless opportunities for exploration and discovery. Whether you're interested in delving into the past, experiencing the vibrancy of the present art scene, or enjoying live performances, Santa Barbara offers a wealth of cultural experiences that enrich the mind and spirit.

ACTIVITIES AND EXPERIENCES

Relaxation and Wellness in Santa Barbara: Spas, Yoga, and Retreats

Santa Barbara, with its serene coastline, gentle climate, and lush landscapes, is a haven for relaxation and wellness. The city and its surroundings offer a wealth of options for those looking to unwind, rejuvenate, and find balance. From luxurious spa resorts and holistic wellness centers to tranquil yoga studios and secluded retreats, Santa Barbara provides a perfect backdrop for nurturing both body and mind.

Spas

Santa Barbara is home to numerous spas that offer a range of services designed to soothe and pamper. These establishments typically combine luxurious settings with a comprehensive menu of treatments:

- **Four Seasons Resort The Biltmore Santa Barbara Spa:** This luxurious spa offers a variety of treatments, including massages, facials, and body wraps, using organic and locally sourced products. Guests can also enjoy the spa's steam rooms, saunas, and private cabanas by the pool for ultimate relaxation.
- **Bacara Resort Spa:** Situated along the picturesque Gaviota Coast, the Bacara Resort Spa provides a holistic wellness experience with treatments inspired by the natural surroundings and the healing powers of the ocean. The spa features an extensive range of services, from traditional massages and facials to innovative therapies like seaweed wraps and saltwater soaks.
- **Salt Cave Santa Barbara:** Offering a unique experience, this spa is built around naturally formed salt caves and provides halotherapy sessions, where the microclimate of the caves is said to have therapeutic and restorative properties. They also offer massages and skin treatments within the serene ambiance of the salt caves.
- **The Spa at El Encanto:** Part of the Belmond El Encanto hotel, this spa offers an idyllic retreat with treatments that blend Eastern and Western techniques, featuring an array of services from massages and facials to body therapies, all within a tranquil, luxurious setting overlooking Santa

Barbara.
- **Alchemie Spa Retreat:** Located in the heart of Santa Barbara, Alchemie provides a holistic approach to wellness with organic spa treatments, including massages, facials, and body scrubs, using eco-friendly and sustainable products in a serene, nurturing environment.
- **Montecito Shores Spa:** Nestled in the exclusive Montecito area, this spa specializes in personalized services, offering luxury treatments like hydrotherapy, aromatherapy massages, and anti-aging facials, catering to those seeking a private and bespoke spa experience.
- **Evolve Wellness Spa:** A wellness sanctuary that offers a comprehensive approach to health and well-being, featuring services like therapeutic massages, acupuncture, and wellness coaching, all aimed at promoting holistic healing and balance.
- **Cielo Spa Boutique:** A boutique spa known for its personalized services and attention to detail, offering a range of treatments from custom facials and massage therapy to waxing and beauty services, set in a peaceful, intimate setting.
- **Float Luxury Spa:** Offering a unique floating therapy alongside traditional spa treatments, Float Luxury Spa provides massages, facials, and body treatments in a calm, ocean-inspired environment, perfect for unwinding and rejuvenating.
-

Yoga

The yoga community in Santa Barbara is vibrant and welcoming, with studios offering classes for all levels and styles, from vigorous Vinyasa flows to gentle restorative sessions:

- **Yoga Soup:** A popular studio in downtown Santa Barbara, Yoga Soup offers a diverse schedule of classes, workshops, and events to foster physical health and spiritual well-being. The studio's eclectic approach ensures something for everyone, from beginners to advanced practitioners.
- **Divinitree Yoga & Art Studio:** This studio combines yoga practice

with artistic expression, providing a creative and nurturing environment for personal growth and community connection. Classes range from dynamic physical practices to calming meditation and mindfulness sessions.
- **Power of Your Om:** This studio is focused on empowering individuals through yoga. It offers a variety of classes that emphasize strength, flexibility, and balance, encouraging a powerful personal practice.
- **CorePower Yoga:** With multiple locations in Santa Barbara, CorePower Yoga offers a range of classes that blend strength, sweat, and spirituality. The studio is known for its heated yoga classes, including CorePower Yoga's signature series, which is designed to provide a challenging and invigorating workout while promoting mental clarity and focus.
- **Santa Barbara Yoga Center:** One of the oldest and most established yoga studios in the area, the Santa Barbara Yoga Center offers a wide variety of yoga styles and classes, including Iyengar, Vinyasa, Hatha, and restorative yoga. The center is dedicated to fostering a sense of community and provides a welcoming environment for students of all levels.
- **The Yoga Shack:** Located in the picturesque Santa Ynez Valley just outside Santa Barbara, The Yoga Shack offers an intimate and peaceful setting for yoga practice. Specializing in Vinyasa and Yin yoga, the studio provides a serene environment where students can deepen their practice while surrounded by natural beauty.

Retreats

For those seeking a deeper immersion in wellness and self-care, Santa Barbara and its environs offer several retreat centers where one can disconnect from daily stress and reconnect with nature and self:

- **White Lotus Foundation Retreat Center:** Nestled in the mountains overlooking Santa Barbara, this retreat center offers yoga retreats, teacher training, and workshops in a serene and picturesque setting. The focus is on holistic health, incorporating yoga, meditation, and nature.

- **Sagrada Wellness:** Located in the rolling hills of San Luis Obispo County, just outside Santa Barbara, Sagrada Wellness offers yoga and wellness retreats in a beautiful, tranquil setting. Their retreats include yoga sessions, guided hikes, and organic meals, providing a perfect getaway for rejuvenation.
- **The Retreat in Laguna:** A short drive from Santa Barbara, this luxury beach retreat offers wellness packages that include yoga, meditation, spa treatments, and nutritional guidance, all set against the stunning backdrop of the Pacific Ocean.
- **Ojai Retreat & Inn:** Located in the nearby Ojai Valley, this retreat offers a tranquil setting for relaxation and renewal. With its stunning views, lush gardens, and quiet ambiance, the Ojai Retreat & Inn provides various workshops, yoga classes, and meditation sessions, promoting peace and well-being in a serene, natural environment.

Whether seeking a day of pampering at a spa, a rejuvenating yoga class, or a transformative wellness retreat, Santa Barbara provides an array of options to promote relaxation, health, and wellbeing. The natural beauty and calming energy of the region make it an ideal destination for those looking to nurture their body, mind, and spirit.

Family Fun in Santa Barbara

Santa Barbara is an ideal destination for families, offering a variety of attractions that are both entertaining and educational. With its stunning natural beauty and commitment to conservation and education, the city provides enriching experiences for children and adults alike. Here's a closer look at some of the top family-friendly attractions in Santa Barbara.

Santa Barbara Zoo

- **Location & Features:** Nestled between the ocean and the Santa Ynez Mountains, the Santa Barbara Zoo is a compact yet diverse zoological

garden home to over 500 animals across 160 species.
- **Exhibits & Programs:** The zoo features engaging exhibits like the African Savanna, home to giraffes and lions, and the Australian Outback, showcasing kangaroos and wallabies. Special programs include animal encounters, feeding opportunities, and educational talks, making wildlife education fun and interactive.
- **Family-Friendly Amenities:** With play areas, a miniature train ride encircling the park, and picnic spots with scenic views, the zoo ensures a memorable day out for families.

Santa Barbara Museum of Natural History Sea Center

- **Location & Exploration:** Positioned on the historic Stearns Wharf, the Sea Center provides an up-close look at marine life from the Santa Barbara Channel.
- **Interactive Exhibits:** Families can enjoy hands-on experiences with sea creatures in the touch tanks, explore the life of the deep sea in the interactive displays, and learn about marine science in a fun and engaging way.
- **Conservation Focus:** The center emphasizes marine conservation, offering insights into the local marine ecosystem and the importance of preserving our oceans for future generations.

Chase Palm Park

- **Scenic Setting:** Located along the waterfront, Chase Palm Park is known for its expansive green spaces, playgrounds, and picturesque ocean views.
- **Family Activities:** The park features a historic carousel, a ship-themed playground, and expansive lawns perfect for picnics, games, and leisurely strolls.
- **Community Events:** Throughout the year, the park hosts family-oriented events like free outdoor concerts, festivals, and children's programs, adding to its appeal as a community gathering spot.

Santa Barbara Botanic Garden

- **Natural Beauty:** Spread across 78 acres, the Botanic Garden is dedicated to California native plants. It showcases the diverse flora of the region in beautifully designed landscapes.
- **Educational Opportunities:** The garden offers families a chance to learn about botany, ecology, and conservation in an immersive environment through walking trails, interactive exhibits, and a variety of educational programs.
- **Activities for Kids:** The garden provides children's workshops, family-friendly tours, and seasonal activities that promote a love of nature and outdoor exploration.

Land and Sea Tours in Santa Barbara

- **Unique Adventure Experience:** Santa Barbara's land and sea tours offer a distinctive way to explore the city's rich history and natural beauty. These tours combine exploring urban landscapes with the allure of oceanic adventures, providing a comprehensive overview of the region's diverse attractions.
- **Tour Features:** Companies like Land Shark Tours utilize amphibious vehicles that travel through historic streets, showcasing landmark buildings and cultural sites, before transitioning into the water for a closer look at the marine environment and coastal views. This seamless journey between land and sea captivates visitors with its novelty and educational value.
- **Educational and Fun:** The tours are designed to be entertaining and informative, making them ideal for families and visitors of all ages. Guides often share fascinating stories and facts about Santa Barbara's history, architecture, and marine life, enhancing the experience with their knowledge and enthusiasm.

ACTIVITIES AND EXPERIENCES

Santa Barbara attractions provide fun and entertainment and foster a deeper appreciation for nature, wildlife, and environmental conservation. Families visiting Santa Barbara can look forward to a delightful mix of learning and leisure, making every trip an enriching experience.

6

Events and Festivals

Annual Highlights in Santa Barbara: Seasonal Events and Festivals

Santa Barbara's calendar is rich with seasonal events and festivals that celebrate the city's culture, natural beauty, and community spirit. From vibrant parades to wine tastings and art shows, there's always something happening in this coastal paradise. Additionally, the region's natural phenomena, like whale watching, provide unique experiences tied to specific times of the year. Here's a detailed guide to some of the annual highlights and seasonal events to plan your trip around in Santa Barbara.

January to March: Winter Whales and Film Fests

Santa Barbara International Film Festival (January/February): The Santa Barbara International Film Festival (SBIFF) is a prestigious and highly anticipated event in the cinematic world, attracting filmmakers, celebrities, industry professionals, and movie enthusiasts from across the globe. Held annually in late January to early February, this 11-day festival transforms Santa Barbara into a bustling hub of cinematic artistry and discussion, showcasing a diverse array of films ranging from international blockbusters to independent and local productions.

Overview and History

- **Establishment:** Founded in 1986, SBIFF has grown exponentially, becoming one of the leading film festivals in the United States.
- **Mission:** The festival aims to celebrate the art of cinema and provide a platform for filmmakers to showcase their work while fostering community engagement and education through film.

Festival Highlights

- **Film Screenings:** SBIFF features screenings of over 200 films, including world premieres, U.S. debuts, and critically acclaimed works across various genres and formats, from feature-length movies to shorts and documentaries.
- **Tribute Awards:** The festival is renowned for its tribute awards, where accomplished actors, directors, and industry luminaries are honored for their contributions to film. Past honorees include renowned figures like Martin Scorsese, Cate Blanchett, and Denzel Washington.
- **Panel Discussions:** SBIFF hosts panels and Q&A sessions with filmmakers, actors, and industry experts, offering insights into the filmmaking process, industry trends, and the creative journeys of those involved in film production.

Educational Programs and Community Engagement

- **10-10-10 Student Filmmaking and Screenwriting Competition:** SBIFF actively supports emerging talent through programs like the 10-10-10 competition, where students and aspiring filmmakers are challenged to create short films within the festival's timeframe.
- **Free Community Events:** The festival includes free screenings and events accessible to the public, ensuring that the joy and appreciation of

film are shared widely within the community.

Venue and Atmosphere

- **Locations:** Screenings and events take place in various historic and contemporary venues across Santa Barbara, including the iconic Arlington Theatre and the modern Riviera Theatre, creating a vibrant and immersive festival atmosphere.
- **Festival Village:** A central hub for festival-goers, the Village offers a place to gather, discuss films, and enjoy food and entertainment, enhancing the communal and festive spirit of the event.

The Santa Barbara International Film Festival not only highlights the city's cultural significance but also contributes to the global film community by providing a platform for innovative storytelling and artistic expression. For film lovers, SBIFF is a not-to-be-missed event that offers a window into the world of cinema in the picturesque setting of Santa Barbara.

Whale Watching Season (February/March): Whale Watching Season in Santa Barbara

Santa Barbara, with its unique geographical position along the California coast, offers one of the most spectacular settings for whale watching. The region's nutrient-rich waters attract a variety of whale species throughout the year, making it a premier destination for enthusiasts and nature lovers. Here's a detailed look at the whale watching season in Santa Barbara.

Prime Season and Species

- **Peak Months:** While whales can be spotted year-round, the peak whale watching season in Santa Barbara runs from late December through mid-April. During this time, the migration patterns of different whale species bring them closer to the shore.
- **Gray Whales:** The winter and early spring months are particularly

notable for the gray whale migration, one of nature's most impressive journeys. These gentle giants travel from the cold Arctic seas to the warm lagoons of Baja California, Mexico, to breed and give birth, passing by Santa Barbara's coastline.
- **Blue and Humpback Whales:** Starting in late spring and continuing through the summer, the area becomes a feeding ground for blue and humpback whales, attracted by the abundant krill and small fish in the Santa Barbara Channel.

Whale Watching Tours

- **Guided Tours:** Numerous operators in Santa Barbara offer whale watching tours, providing expert commentary and guidance to enhance the experience. These tours are conducted on specially designed boats that can navigate the waters with minimal disturbance to the wildlife.
- **Best Practices:** Reputable tour companies adhere to strict guidelines to ensure responsible wildlife viewing, maintaining a safe distance to avoid disrupting the whales' natural behaviors.

Educational and Conservation Aspects

- **Marine Education:** Many tours incorporate educational elements, teaching passengers about the marine ecosystem, whale behaviors, and conservation efforts to protect these majestic creatures and their habitat.
- **Research and Conservation:** Some tour operators collaborate with marine research organizations, contributing to ongoing studies and conservation initiatives. Participants on these tours may have the unique opportunity to engage with marine biologists and researchers.

What to Expect

- **Viewing Experience:** While sightings can vary, common experiences include watching gray whales breach or spy-hop and observing humpback

whales' acrobatics and tail slapping. The sight of blue whales, the largest animals on the planet, is an awe-inspiring experience.
- **Other Marine Life:** In addition to whales, viewers often spot dolphins, sea lions, seals, and a variety of seabirds, making the trip a comprehensive marine wildlife experience.

Tips for a Great Whale Watching Experience

- **Timing:** Early morning tours often offer calmer sea conditions and better visibility.
- **Preparation:** Dressing in layers is recommended, as temperatures can be cooler on the water. Bringing binoculars, sunscreen, and motion sickness remedies can enhance the comfort and enjoyment of the trip.

Whale watching in Santa Barbara is not just an activity; it's an immersive experience that connects individuals with the majesty of the marine environment, offering a deeper appreciation for the natural world and the importance of preserving it for future generations.

April to June: Flowers and Flavors

Santa Barbara Earth Day Festival (April): The Santa Barbara Earth Day Festival is a dynamic and impactful event that celebrates environmental stewardship, sustainability, and community activism. Held annually around Earth Day in April, this festival has grown into one of the largest and most comprehensive environmental gatherings in the region, attracting thousands of visitors each year. Here's a detailed look at what makes the Santa Barbara Earth Day Festival a must-attend event for those passionate about the planet.
Origins and Mission

- **Historical Significance:** Inspired by the national Earth Day movement that began in 1970, Santa Barbara's Earth Day Festival was initiated

following the devastating oil spill off its coast in 1969, sparking local and national environmental activism.
- **Purpose:** The festival aims to educate, inspire, and empower individuals and communities to protect and improve the environment, promoting a sustainable and healthy future for all.

Festival Highlights

- **Exhibitors and Booths:** Featuring over 200 exhibitors, the festival showcases a wide range of environmental organizations, green businesses, and community groups. Attendees can learn about renewable energy, sustainable agriculture, water conservation, and much more.
- **Educational Workshops and Speakers:** The event hosts a variety of workshops, presentations, and panel discussions led by experts, activists, and thought leaders in the environmental field. Topics cover a broad spectrum of issues, including climate change, conservation, renewable energy, and eco-friendly living.
- **Live Entertainment:** The festival features multiple stages with live music, dance performances, and artistic displays, celebrating the arts as a powerful medium for environmental messaging and community engagement.
- **Activities for All Ages:** With a dedicated Kids' Zone offering eco-friendly crafts, games, and educational activities, the festival is family-friendly and encourages environmental awareness from a young age.
- **Green Car Show:** A highlight of the festival, the Green Car Show displays the latest in electric and hybrid vehicle technology, allowing attendees to explore and test drive the newest models and innovations in sustainable transportation.

Sustainability Practices

- **Zero Waste Goals:** The festival emphasizes waste reduction, recycling, and composting, aiming to be a zero-waste event. Visitors are encouraged

to bring reusable water bottles, bags, and utensils to minimize single-use plastics and waste.
- **Local and Organic Foods:** Food vendors at the festival offer a variety of local, organic, and vegetarian/vegan options, highlighting sustainable food practices and promoting healthy, environmentally friendly eating choices.

Community Impact and Legacy

- **Environmental Advocacy:** Beyond the festivities, the Earth Day Festival serves as a platform for environmental advocacy, providing resources and opportunities for attendees to get involved in local and global sustainability efforts.
- **Legacy of Activism:** The festival continues to embody Santa Barbara's pioneering spirit in environmental activism, inspiring new generations to champion the cause of conservation and sustainability.

The Santa Barbara Earth Day Festival is more than just an annual event; it's a vital expression of the community's longstanding commitment to environmental preservation and sustainability. Offering a blend of education, activism, and celebration, the festival engages the hearts and minds of participants, fostering a collective resolve to protect our planet for future generations.

Santa Barbara County Vintners Festival (April): The Santa Barbara County Vintners Festival is a premier event in the wine calendar, celebrating the exceptional viticulture and winemaking of the region. This annual festival, typically held in April, marks the beginning of the spring season and offers wine enthusiasts an opportunity to explore the diverse and abundant offerings of Santa Barbara County's wine country.

Festival Overview

- **Location and Setting:** The festival takes place in various picturesque locations throughout Santa Barbara County, showcasing the natural beauty and diversity of the wine-growing regions. From rolling hills and coastal vistas to charming vineyards, the settings provide a perfect backdrop for the wine-centric celebrations.

- **Participating Wineries:** Featuring over 100 local wineries, the festival offers an extensive range of wines, representing the various appellations and grape varieties that make Santa Barbara County a unique wine destination. Attendees can taste wines from established producers as well as discover offerings from newer, boutique wineries.

Experiences and Activities

- **Wine Tastings:** The heart of the festival is the grand tasting event, where guests can sample an impressive array of wines, including rare and limited-edition vintages. Winemakers and vineyard representatives are often on hand to discuss their wines, providing insights into their production methods and the characteristics of their specific terroirs.
- **Educational Seminars and Workshops:** The festival often includes educational components, such as seminars, workshops, and panel discussions led by wine experts, sommeliers, and industry professionals. These sessions cover topics ranging from viticulture and winemaking techniques to wine pairing and tasting nuances.
- **Culinary Delights:** In addition to the wine offerings, the festival features gourmet food from some of the area's top chefs and local culinary artisans. Food pairings, cooking demonstrations, and specialty food booths highlight the region's rich agricultural bounty and culinary excellence.
- **Live Entertainment and Art:** Music, live bands, and artistic displays add a festive atmosphere to the event, with performances ranging from jazz and classical to contemporary music, enhancing the overall experience of the festival.

Community and Sustainability

- **Support for Local Economy:** The festival not only celebrates Santa Barbara's winemaking achievements but also supports the local economy, spotlighting small businesses, artisans, and farmers.
- **Sustainability Initiatives:** Many participating wineries and vendors showcase their commitment to sustainable practices, from organic and biodynamic farming to water conservation and eco-friendly packaging.

Planning Your Visit

- **Ticketing and Packages:** The festival offers various ticketing options, including general admission, VIP experiences, and weekend packages that may include exclusive tastings, vineyard tours, and special events.
- **Accommodations and Transportation:** Visitors are encouraged to plan their accommodations early, as the festival attracts a large number of guests. Many local hotels offer special rates and packages for festival-goers, and shuttle services are often available to ensure safe and convenient transportation to and from the event.

The Santa Barbara County Vintners Festival is an essential experience for wine lovers. It offers a comprehensive and enjoyable way to explore the flavors, people, and landscapes that define Santa Barbara's wine culture. This celebration not only provides pleasure and education to its attendees but also fosters a sense of community and appreciation for the art and science of winemaking.

I Madonnari Italian Street Painting Festival (May)

The I Madonnari Italian Street Painting Festival is a vibrant celebration of both the visual arts and Italian culture, taking place annually over Memorial Day weekend in Santa Barbara. Set against the picturesque backdrop of the Old Mission Santa Barbara, this event transforms the mission's plaza into a kaleidoscope of color and creativity, drawing artists, residents, and tourists to partake in a unique artistic tradition.

Festival Origins and Inspiration

- **Historical Roots:** Modeled after the Italian tradition of street painting, I Madonnari honors the practice of madonnari, artists who would create chalk masterpieces on the pavement.
- **Cultural Exchange:** Introduced to Santa Barbara in the late 1980s, the festival has since become a beloved community event, showcasing the rich cultural ties between Santa Barbara and Italy.

Artistic Showcase and Community Engagement

- **Street Art Creation:** Artists from around the world converge on the mission's grounds to create large-scale chalk murals, transforming the asphalt and concrete surfaces into stunning works of art.
- **Interactive Experience:** Spectators can watch the artworks come to life and engage with the artists, gaining insight into their creative processes and the stories behind their designs.

Educational and Charitable Aspects

- **Youth Involvement:** The festival includes a special section for young artists, which provides schoolchildren with the opportunity to participate and express their creativity on the pavement.
- **Fundraising Goals:** I Madonnari serves as a fundraiser for the Children's Creative Project, a nonprofit arts education program, highlighting the festival's commitment to supporting arts in the community.

Culinary and Musical Elements

- **Italian Cuisine:** In keeping with its Italian theme, the festival features food stalls offering traditional Italian dishes, from pizza and pasta to gelato, allowing attendees to savor the flavors of Italy.
- **Live Performances:** Musical and dance performances add to the festive atmosphere, with local and international acts providing entertainment throughout the event.

Legacy and Impact

- **Cultural Staple:** I Madonnari has become a significant cultural event in Santa Barbara, celebrated for its ability to bring together art, education, and community in a dynamic and accessible way.
- **Tourist Attraction:** The festival not only enriches the local cultural scene but also attracts visitors from across the globe, contributing to the city's tourism and international cultural exchange.

I Madonnari Italian Street Painting Festival is a testament to the power of public art and community collaboration, offering a space where creativity, tradition, and cultural appreciation come together in a spectacular display. It provides a tangible connection to the Italian origins of street painting while celebrating the artistic spirit and communal values of Santa Barbara.

Summer Solstice Parade (June): The Summer Solstice Parade in Santa Barbara is an annual celebration that marks the longest day of the year. It embodies the vibrant spirit and artistic flair of the local community. This colorful and lively event, taking place in June, is one of the city's most beloved and anticipated festivals, drawing thousands of spectators and participants worldwide.

Origins and Significance

- **Historical Background:** The Santa Barbara Summer Solstice Parade began in the 1970s as a small, informal event and has since evolved into a major cultural celebration, reflecting the diverse and creative community of the city.
- **Celebration of Light and Life:** The parade symbolizes the onset of summer, celebrating the sun, light, and the fertility of the earth, embracing themes of renewal, growth, and community spirit.

Parade Highlights

- **Vibrant Procession:** The parade features a spectacular array of floats, costumes, and performances, all created by local artists, community groups, and volunteers. The floats are known for their imaginative and elaborate designs, often featuring kinetic sculptures, intricate papier-mâché art, and interactive elements.
- **Performers and Musicians:** Dancers, acrobats, musicians, and performers in dazzling costumes bring the streets to life with their dynamic routines and infectious energy. The parade's open and inclusive atmosphere encourages participation from diverse groups, celebrating the cultural richness of Santa Barbara.
- **Thematic Expression:** Each year, the parade is centered around a specific theme, which guides the creation of the floats and costumes, adding depth and narrative to the visual spectacle. Themes are often inspired by nature, mythology, art, and social issues, allowing for a creative and thoughtful exploration of various concepts.

Festival Activities

- **Alameda Park Celebration:** Following the parade, the celebration continues in Alameda Park, where attendees can enjoy live music, dance performances, and interactive art installations. The park becomes a hub of activity, with food vendors, craft stalls, and family-friendly activities, creating a festive and communal atmosphere.
- **Art Workshops and Community Engagement:** In the weeks leading up to the parade, the community is invited to participate in art workshops and build sessions, where they can contribute to the parade's floats and costumes, fostering a sense of ownership and collective creativity.

Impact and Legacy

- **Cultural Impact:** The Summer Solstice Parade is not just a festive event but a vital part of Santa Barbara's cultural identity, showcasing the city's commitment to the arts, community engagement, and environmental

awareness.
- **Tourist Attraction:** As one of the largest and most colorful festivals in the region, the parade attracts tourists from across the globe, boosting the local economy and highlighting Santa Barbara as a destination for cultural tourism.
- The Summer Solstice Parade in Santa Barbara is more than an event; it's a dynamic expression of community, artistry, and celebration, encapsulating the essence of the city's cultural vibrancy and collective spirit. Whether as a participant or a spectator, the parade offers an unforgettable experience of joy, creativity, and unity in the heart of one of California's most picturesque cities.

July to September: Summer Fun and Cultural Celebrations

Fourth of July Fireworks and Festival: The Fourth of July Fireworks and Festival in Santa Barbara is a quintessential celebration of American independence, combining patriotic spirit with community festivities. This event, held annually on July 4th, is a highlight of the summer season in Santa Barbara, offering a day of family-friendly activities, entertainment, and a spectacular fireworks display over the beach.

Festival Activities and Entertainment

- **Daytime Celebrations:** The festivities begin in the morning with a variety of activities across the city. Parks and public spaces host family picnics, live music, and games, creating a festive atmosphere. The waterfront and downtown areas become bustling hubs of activity, with food vendors, arts and crafts stalls, and street performances.
- **Parade and Performances:** A traditional Fourth of July parade features marching bands, floats, and community groups, showcasing local culture and patriotism. Throughout the day, stages set up in key locations offer live music and dance performances, ranging from classic rock and pop to folk and jazz, reflecting the diverse musical tastes of the community.

EVENTS AND FESTIVALS

Fireworks Display

- **Spectacular Show:** As the sun sets, all eyes turn to the night sky for the main attraction: the fireworks display. Launched from West Beach, the fireworks illuminate the night with vibrant colors and patterns, creating a breathtaking spectacle over the Santa Barbara coastline.
- **Viewing Locations:** Prime viewing spots include the beachfront, Stearns Wharf, and higher vantage points around the city. Many residents and visitors gather early to secure the best locations, bringing blankets and beach chairs to enjoy the show.

Community and Cultural Significance

- **Community Spirit:** The Fourth of July celebration in Santa Barbara is a testament to the strong sense of community and patriotism in the city. Residents and visitors of all ages come together to celebrate, reflecting the city's inclusive and celebratory spirit.
- **Cultural Traditions:** The event also serves as a reminder of Santa Barbara's rich history and cultural heritage, with historical reenactments and educational exhibits often part of the festivities, offering insights into the nation's past and the principles of independence and freedom.

Planning and Participation

- **Preparation and Safety:** City authorities and event organizers ensure that the celebrations are safe and enjoyable for everyone, with increased security measures and safety protocols in place. Attendees are encouraged to be mindful of their surroundings and to respect local regulations and guidelines.
- **Community Involvement:** Local businesses, nonprofit organizations, and volunteers play a significant role in the success of the event, contributing to its vibrant and communal atmosphere. The festival provides an opportunity for local artisans and entrepreneurs to showcase

- their products and services, enhancing the community-oriented nature of the celebration.
- The Fourth of July Fireworks and Festival in Santa Barbara encapsulates the joy and pride of American Independence Day, set against the backdrop of one of California's most beautiful coastal cities. With its blend of traditional festivities, community engagement, and spectacular fireworks, it offers a memorable experience that celebrates the spirit of freedom and unity.

Santa Barbara Greek Festival (July)

The Santa Barbara Greek Festival is a vibrant celebration of Greek culture, heritage, and community, held annually in July at Oak Park. This two-day event, one of the city's most festive and joyous occasions, immerses attendees in the rich traditions of Greece, offering a lively weekend of music, dance, food, and familial warmth.

Cultural Celebration and Heritage

- **Time of Year:** Taking place in mid-July, the festival coincides with warm summer weather, perfect for an outdoor cultural celebration.
- **Authentic Experience:** The Greek Festival brings a taste of Greece to Santa Barbara, showcasing traditional customs, attire, and arts, allowing visitors to experience the Hellenic way of life.

Festival Highlights

- **Live Entertainment:** The festival features live Greek music and performances by dancers in traditional costumes, displaying the vibrant and dynamic nature of Greek folk dances.
- **Culinary Delights:** Attendees can savor authentic Greek cuisine, from gyros and souvlaki to baklava and loukoumades, all prepared by local Greek community members and vendors, offering a culinary journey through Greece's diverse flavors.

Cultural and Educational Aspects

- **Cultural Exhibits:** Educational exhibits and booths provide insights into Greek history, art, and the Orthodox Christian faith, offering a deeper understanding of Greek cultural and religious traditions.
- **Language and Workshops:** Language workshops and cultural demonstrations, such as cooking classes and craft making, allow participants to engage actively with Greek customs and traditions.

Community Involvement and Family-Friendly Atmosphere

- **Volunteerism:** The festival is largely run by volunteers from the local Greek community, emphasizing the importance of communal effort and cultural pride.
- **Activities for All Ages:** With a dedicated area for children's games and activities, the festival ensures a fun and engaging experience for younger attendees, making it a family-friendly event.

Economic and Social Benefits

- **Support for Local Community:** Proceeds from the festival often go towards supporting local charities and community projects, showcasing the Greek community's commitment to philanthropy and social responsibility.
- **Tourism and Local Economy:** As a popular event in Santa Barbara's cultural calendar, the Greek Festival attracts visitors from across the region, boosting local tourism and benefiting the economy.

The Santa Barbara Greek Festival is more than just an event; it's a heartfelt celebration of Greek culture, offering a space where tradition and community converge in a joyful and welcoming atmosphere. It provides a unique opportunity for both the Greek community and the city at large to come together, celebrating and sharing the rich cultural tapestry that Greece offers.

Old Spanish Days Fiesta (August): Old Spanish Days Fiesta in Santa Barbara is a vibrant celebration of the city's rich Spanish heritage and cultural history. This annual event, taking place on the first Wednesday of August and runs through Sunday, is one of Santa Barbara's oldest and most cherished traditions, drawing locals and visitors alike to partake in a week-long festivity that includes colorful parades, traditional music and dance performances, and a variety of cultural activities.

Historical Background and Significance

- **Origins:** Established in the 1920s, Old Spanish Days Fiesta seeks to honor and preserve Santa Barbara's Spanish, Mexican, and early American roots, reflecting the multicultural history that shapes the region's identity.
- **Cultural Celebration:** The fiesta serves as a living history, showcasing the customs, crafts, cuisine, and performing arts that define the Spanish and Mexican eras of California, promoting cultural awareness and community pride.

Events and Festivities

- **Parades:** The Fiesta Historical Parade is a highlight, featuring beautiful floats, equestrian units, and historical reenactments, making it one of the largest equestrian parades in the United States. The Children's Parade, organized by the local community, allows younger participants to showcase their costumes and cultural pride.
- **Dance and Music:** Flamenco, folklórico, and other traditional dance performances take center stage, with dancers in colorful costumes performing at various venues throughout the city. Live music, ranging from mariachi to classical Spanish guitar, fills the air, enhancing the festive atmosphere.
- **Mercado:** The traditional mercados in downtown Santa Barbara offer authentic Spanish and Mexican cuisine, arts, and crafts. These bustling marketplaces are a feast for the senses, with vendors selling everything

from handmade items to savory dishes and sweet treats.
- **Santa Barbara Rodeo:** An annual event that captures the spirit of the American West, the Santa Barbara Rodeo showcases traditional rodeo competitions like bull riding, barrel racing, and roping. This exciting celebration of cowboy culture features skilled athletes, live entertainment, and family-friendly activities, making it a thrilling experience for attendees of all ages.

Cultural and Educational Impact

- **Preservation of Heritage:** Old Spanish Days Fiesta plays a crucial role in preserving and celebrating the cultural heritage of the region, providing a platform for artists, musicians, and community members to express and sustain their traditions.
- **Educational Opportunities:** The fiesta offers educational experiences for all ages, with activities and displays teaching about the historical and cultural influences of California's Spanish and Mexican periods.

Community Involvement and Participation

- **Volunteerism and Engagement:** The event is brought to life by the efforts of countless volunteers and local organizations, emphasizing a sense of community and collective heritage.
- **Inclusivity:** While rooted in specific cultural traditions, the fiesta welcomes people of all backgrounds to celebrate and learn about Santa Barbara's history and traditions, fostering a sense of inclusivity and mutual respect.

Economic and Social Benefits

- **Tourism and Economy:** One of Santa Barbara's largest and most popular events, Old Spanish Days Fiesta, significantly boosts the local economy by attracting tourists and promoting local businesses.

- **Social Cohesion:** The fiesta strengthens community bonds and fosters residents' sense of belonging and pride, reinforcing social ties and cultural identity.

Old Spanish Days Fiesta in Santa Barbara is more than just a festival; it's a vibrant celebration of the city's historical roots and cultural diversity. Through its array of events and activities, the fiesta offers a dynamic and engaging way for residents and visitors to connect with the past, celebrate the present, and pass on traditions to future generations.

Santa Barbara French Festival (July): The Santa Barbara French Festival is a vibrant celebration of French culture, held annually in July. This event, one of the largest French festivals in the Western United States, transforms Oak Park in Santa Barbara into a lively tableau of French music, dance, and gastronomy, drawing thousands of visitors for a weekend of Francophile fun and festivity.
Festival Highlights

- **Cultural Performances:** The festival features multiple stages where attendees can enjoy a variety of live performances, including traditional and contemporary French music, dance troupes performing styles from can-can to folk dances, and theatrical acts that bring French culture and history to life.
- **Cuisine and Wine:** Culinary delights are at the heart of the French Festival, with vendors offering an array of French specialties such as crêpes, pastries, escargot, and baguettes, along with regional dishes from various parts of France. Wine enthusiasts can savor French wines and champagne, providing a taste of France's renowned vineyards.
- **Art and Crafts:** Artisans display and sell various French-themed goods, from handmade jewelry and clothing to artwork and home décor. These market stalls offer unique shopping opportunities and showcase French culture's craftsmanship and artistic traditions.

Educational and Cultural Aspects

- **Language and Workshops:** The festival often includes language workshops and cultural presentations, offering attendees the chance to learn basic French phrases or delve deeper into the country's history, art, and cultural nuances.
- **Children's Activities:** Family-friendly activities, such as puppet shows, face painting, and games, ensure that even the youngest visitors can engage in the festivities and learn about French culture in a fun and interactive environment.

Community and Celebration

- **Community Gathering:** The French Festival serves as a gathering point for the local French community and Francophiles, fostering a sense of camaraderie and cultural exchange. It's an opportunity for people of all backgrounds to experience and celebrate French culture.
- **Entertainment and Atmosphere:** With its festive atmosphere, complete with decorations in the colors of the French flag and the sounds of French music filling the air, the festival offers a joyful and immersive experience that feels like a mini vacation to France.

Impact and Legacy

- **Cultural Appreciation:** The festival significantly promotes cultural appreciation and understanding, highlighting the diversity and richness of French culture and its influence on the world.
- **Economic and Social Benefits:** Beyond the cultural experience, the festival benefits the local economy by supporting small businesses and attracting tourists to Santa Barbara while also providing a fun and educational event for the community.

The Santa Barbara French Festival is a testament to the city's vibrant cultural scene and ability to unite people in celebration of global traditions. Offering a slice of French life, complete with its art, cuisine, and joie de vivre, the festival is a cherished event that locals and visitors alike look forward to every year.

October to December: Harvest and Holidays

Harbor & Seafood Festival (October): The Santa Barbara Harbor & Seafood Festival is an eagerly anticipated annual event celebrating the local seafood industry and maritime heritage. Held in October, coinciding with the opening of lobster season, this festival at the Santa Barbara Harbor attracts seafood lovers and families for a day of fresh catch, cooking demonstrations, and nautical activities.

Fresh Seafood and Culinary Delights

- **Local Seafood:** The festival is a seafood enthusiast's dream, offering an array of freshly caught offerings like lobster, crab, oysters, and sea urchins, provided directly by local fishermen.
- **Cooking Demonstrations:** Renowned local chefs showcase their culinary skills in live cooking demonstrations, preparing seafood dishes while sharing tips and recipes with attendees. These sessions educate and entertain, highlighting the versatility and flavor of fresh, local seafood.

Maritime Exhibits and Activities

- **Maritime Education:** The festival provides exhibits about marine life, sustainable fishing practices, and the importance of preserving ocean ecosystems. Local marine organizations, including research institutes and conservation groups, participate in the festival to share knowledge and engage with the community.
- **Boat Tours and Displays:** Attendees can explore Santa Barbara's maritime heritage through boat tours, including visits to working fishing

boats, and displays of maritime equipment and technology.

Family-Friendly Entertainment

- **Live Music and Performances:** The festival features live bands and performers, creating a lively and festive atmosphere. Music ranges from local bands playing a variety of genres to traditional maritime songs that echo the harbor's history.
- **Children's Activities:** The event is family-friendly, with activities designed for children, such as face painting, nautical-themed crafts, and interactive educational stations, making it enjoyable for all ages.

Community and Sustainability

- **Support for Local Fishermen:** The Harbor & Seafood Festival highlights and supports the local fishing community, providing a platform for fishermen to sell their catch directly to the public and share their knowledge and experiences.
- **Sustainability Focus:** The event emphasizes sustainable seafood and responsible fishing practices, educating the public on how to make environmentally friendly seafood choices.

Festival Atmosphere and Experience

- **Scenic Location:** Set against the picturesque Santa Barbara Harbor backdrop, the festival offers stunning ocean views, making it an ideal location for a seafood celebration.
- **Community Spirit:** The festival is a testament to Santa Barbara's community spirit and its connection to the sea, bringing together residents, visitors, fishermen, and maritime enthusiasts in a shared appreciation for the ocean's bounty.

The Santa Barbara Harbor & Seafood Festival is more than just an event; it celebrates the region's rich maritime culture and seafood industry, offering a day of delicious food, educational experiences, and family fun. For those who cherish the flavors of the sea and the stories of those who harvest it, this festival is an annual highlight not to be missed.

Santa Barbara International Orchid Show (October): The Santa Barbara International Orchid Show is one of the oldest and largest orchid exhibitions in the United States, celebrating the beauty, diversity, and artistic appeal of orchids. Held annually in March, this event transforms the Earl Warren Showgrounds in Santa Barbara into an orchid paradise, attracting orchid enthusiasts, botanists, and floral artists from around the world.

Exhibition Highlights

- **Orchid Displays:** The show features thousands of orchids in spectacular displays, showcasing a wide variety of species and hybrids. Renowned growers, both local and international, exhibit their finest specimens, competing for awards in various categories.
- **Themed Gardens:** Each year, the show presents themed garden displays, creatively arranged to highlight the orchids' natural beauty and versatility in landscaping and garden design. These immersive environments offer inspiration for hobbyists and professionals alike.

Educational Opportunities

- **Cultivation Workshops:** Attendees can participate in workshops and seminars led by orchid experts, covering topics such as care, cultivation, and propagation techniques. These sessions provide valuable insights for both novice growers and experienced collectors.
- **Docent Tours:** Guided tours offer a deeper understanding of the orchids on display, with experts sharing information about the plants' origins, ecological roles, and conservation status.

Market and Artistry

- **Orchid Sales:** The festival includes a large sales area where visitors can purchase orchids, growing supplies, and related merchandise. This market provides a unique opportunity to acquire rare and exotic orchids not commonly available in commercial nurseries.
- **Art and Photography:** The show often features art and photography exhibitions, where artists and photographers display their orchid-inspired works, capturing the intricate beauty of these flowers in various artistic mediums.

Community and Cultural Impact

- **Networking and Collaboration:** The show serves as a networking hub for orchid societies, hobbyists, and professionals, fostering collaboration and sharing of knowledge within the orchid-growing community.
- **Cultural Significance:** As a long-standing event in Santa Barbara's cultural calendar, the Orchid Show highlights the city's horticultural heritage and its role in the international orchid cultivation scene.

Visitor Experience

- **Festival Atmosphere:** Beyond the exhibits, the show features a festive atmosphere with food vendors, live music, and cultural performances, making it an enjoyable event for the whole family.
- **Orchid Care and Education:** For those new to orchid care, the show offers a wealth of resources and expert advice, helping to demystify the process of growing these exotic plants.

The Santa Barbara International Orchid Show is not just a display of floral beauty but a comprehensive event that celebrates the art, science, and passion behind orchid cultivation. It provides a fascinating and educational experience for all visitors, from seasoned orchid enthusiasts to those simply captivated by the allure of these extraordinary flowers.

Day of the Dead (Día de los Muertos) in Santa Barbara (Oct/Nov): The Day of the Dead, or Día de los Muertos, is a deeply significant cultural and spiritual celebration observed in Santa Barbara, typically taking place at the end of October through the beginning of November. This event honors the memory of deceased loved ones, blending indigenous Mexican traditions with contemporary cultural elements, and creating a vibrant tapestry of rituals, art, and community gatherings.

Cultural Significance and Traditions

- **Historical Roots:** Originating from ancient Mesoamerican rituals combined with Catholic influences, Día de los Muertos is a time when the veil between the living and the dead is believed to be the thinnest, allowing for a reunion and celebration of the deceased.
- **Altars and Offerings:** Central to the celebration are the ofrendas, or altars, adorned with photos, candles, marigolds (cempasúchil), incense, and offerings of food, drinks, and personal items that the departed enjoyed in life, symbolizing welcome and respect for the spirits.

Events and Activities

- **Community Altars:** Public spaces in Santa Barbara, such as museums, cultural centers, and parks, host elaborate community altars where individuals and groups contribute memorials, creating a collective space for remembrance and homage.
- **Art and Workshops:** The celebration includes art exhibitions, workshops, and presentations that explore the themes of mortality and celebration of life, often featuring traditional crafts like sugar skull decorating and papel picado making.

Performances and Parades

- **Music and Dance:** Traditional Mexican music and folkloric dance performances are central to the festivities, with mariachi bands and ballet

folklórico troupes bringing the stories and themes of Día de los Muertos to life.
- **Processions and Costume:** Parades or processions, often featuring participants in calavera (skull) makeup and costumes, weave through the streets, symbolizing the journey of the souls between the worlds.

Culinary Aspects

- **Festive Foods:** Special foods are an integral part of the celebration, including pan de muerto (bread of the dead), tamales, and other dishes that are placed on altars and shared among families and friends in a communal feast.

Educational and Communal Impact

- **Cultural Education:** The celebration serves as an educational opportunity, teaching the community and visitors about the traditions, symbolism, and cultural importance of Día de los Muertos.
- **Community Healing and Unity:** By openly acknowledging grief and celebrating the lives of the departed, Día de los Muertos in Santa Barbara fosters a sense of unity, healing, and respect for cultural heritage and diversity.

Day of the Dead in Santa Barbara is not just a cultural event; it's a profound communal expression of memory, heritage, and life affirmation. Through its colorful altars, poignant art, and joyful celebrations, Día de los Muertos bridges the past and present, inviting everyone to partake in a tradition that honors life and the eternal bond with those who have passed.

Holiday Parades and Markets (December): Santa Barbara celebrates the holiday season with a series of festive parades and markets that capture the joy and spirit of this special time of year. These events bring the community together and offer visitors a chance to experience the city's unique blend of traditional and coastal holiday festivities.

Holiday Parades

- **Downtown Holiday Parade:** A cherished tradition, this parade lights up State Street with a procession of colorful floats, marching bands, performance groups, and community groups, all centered around a festive theme. Santa Claus often makes an appearance, delighting children and adults alike.
- **Parade of Lights at the Harbor:** Santa Barbara's waterfront sparkles during the Parade of Lights, where boats adorned with festive lights and decorations sail along the coast. This nautical parade culminates in a spectacular fireworks display, reflecting over the water and adding to the magic of the evening.

Holiday Markets

- **Santa Barbara Arts and Crafts Show:** During the holiday season, this weekly show along Cabrillo Boulevard transforms into a festive market. Local artists and craftsmen sell unique, handcrafted gifts, including jewelry, paintings, pottery, and more, perfect for holiday shopping.
- **Holiday Pop-Up Markets:** Various pop-up holiday markets and fairs occur throughout Santa Barbara, featuring artisan goods, gourmet food items, and holiday decor. These markets often include live music, food vendors, and activities for children, creating a festive shopping experience.

Festive Activities and Attractions

- **Seasonal Performances:** The holiday season in Santa Barbara is marked by an array of cultural performances, including ballets like "The Nutcracker," holiday concerts, and theater productions, adding a touch of artistic flair to the festivities.
- **Holiday Light Displays:** Neighborhoods and businesses throughout

the city showcase elaborate holiday light displays and decorations, with some areas becoming local attractions for their festive and creative presentations.

Community and Charity Events

- **Charitable Activities:** Many holiday events in Santa Barbara support local charities and causes, providing opportunities for attendees to give back through toy drives, food donations, and fundraising activities.
- **Community Gatherings:** From tree-lighting ceremonies to holiday-themed workshops and Santa meet-and-greets, there are numerous community events that offer fun and festive ways to celebrate the season with family and friends.

The holiday parades and markets in Santa Barbara are more than just annual events; they are a vibrant expression of the community's festive spirit and generosity. Offering a blend of traditional holiday cheer and the relaxed ambiance of the Californian coast, these celebrations create a delightful and heartwarming atmosphere that makes the holiday season in Santa Barbara truly special.

These events and many others throughout the year highlight Santa Barbara's diverse cultural fabric and offer visitors a chance to engage with the local community and traditions. Whether you're drawn to the arts, interested in nature, or looking to celebrate with the locals, Santa Barbara's annual highlights enrich travelers' experiences.

7

Planning Your Trip

Accommodations in Santa Barbara: From Luxury Resorts to Cozy Bed and Breakfasts

Santa Barbara offers a diverse range of accommodations to suit every preference and budget, from opulent luxury resorts to quaint bed and breakfasts. Here's a selection of 15 options that highlight the variety available, spanning affordable to high-end choices.

Luxury Resorts

1. **Four Seasons Resort The Biltmore Santa Barbara**: Nestled along the pristine beaches of Montecito, this luxury resort offers elegant accommodations, a world-class spa, and fine dining, set in lush, tropical gardens.
2. **The Ritz-Carlton Bacara, Santa Barbara**: With stunning ocean views, this upscale resort features luxurious rooms and suites, multiple swimming pools, a spa, and access to beautiful beaches.
3. **Belmond El Encanto**: Perched in the hills, offering panoramic views of the city and ocean, this iconic property provides a serene retreat with exquisite rooms, a spa, and fine dining.

Boutique Hotels

1. **Hotel Californian**: Located in the Funk Zone, this stylish hotel combines modern luxury with Spanish Colonial Revival architecture and is close to beaches and urban wine-tasting rooms.
2. **Kimpton Canary Hotel**: Offering a rooftop pool with spectacular views, this downtown hotel blends upscale amenities with the warmth and style of a boutique property.

Mid-Range Hotels

1. **The Wayfarer**: Situated in the vibrant Funk Zone, this trendy hotel/hostel hybrid offers private and shared accommodations, making it a chic yet budget-friendly option.
2. **Harbor House Inn**: A short walk from West Beach, this charming inn provides individually decorated rooms with kitchenettes, ideal for longer stays and those who prefer a homey feel.
3. **Hotel Milo Santa Barbara**: Located along the waterfront, this hotel offers comfortable accommodations with access to beaches, wharfs, and downtown attractions.

Budget-Friendly Options

1. **Agave Inn**: A boutique motel that offers an affordable stay with a touch of style, featuring uniquely decorated rooms inspired by the vibrant culture of Santa Barbara.
2. **The Presidio**: This budget-conscious hotel is located in downtown Santa Barbara, providing simple, comfortable rooms close to shops, restaurants, and historic sites.

Bed and Breakfasts

1. **Simpson House Inn**: Nestled in a historic estate, this bed and breakfast

is known for its elegant rooms, lush gardens, and gourmet breakfast, offering a peaceful and romantic getaway.
2. **Cheshire Cat Inn**: With cozy, Alice in Wonderland-themed rooms and beautiful gardens, this B&B provides a whimsical and welcoming atmosphere.
3. **The Eagle Inn**: A short walk from the beach, this charming inn offers comfortable accommodations with a friendly, personal touch, ideal for a relaxing coastal stay.

Vacation Rentals and Unique Stays

1. **Santa Barbara Beachfront Rentals**: For those preferring a more private or extended stay, various beachfront properties offer the perfect retreat with stunning views and full amenities.
2. **AutoCamp Santa Barbara**: For a unique lodging experience, AutoCamp offers luxury Airstream trailers in a chic, outdoor setting, combining the fun of camping with modern comforts.

Santa Barbara's accommodations reflect the city's diverse charm and natural beauty, providing options for every type of traveler. Whether seeking luxury and pampering at a resort, the personalized touch of a bed and breakfast, or the convenience and value of a hotel or vacation rental, visitors are sure to find the perfect place to stay in this picturesque coastal city.

Transportation in Santa Barbara County: Navigating by Car, Public Transport, and Bike

Santa Barbara County offers a variety of transportation options to suit different preferences and needs, making it easy to explore the region's scenic beauty, cultural attractions, and recreational spots. Whether you prefer driving, taking public transport, or cycling, here's how you can navigate Santa Barbara County effectively.

By Car

- **Rental Services:** Numerous rental car agencies operate at the Santa Barbara Airport and throughout the city, offering a range of vehicles from economy cars to luxury models.
- **Scenic Drives:** Driving is a fantastic way to discover the county, with scenic routes like the Pacific Coast Highway offering breathtaking ocean views and access to remote beaches and hiking trails.
- **Parking:** Downtown Santa Barbara has ample parking, including lots, garages, and street parking, though it's wise to be mindful of posted restrictions and time limits.

Public Transport

- **Santa Barbara Metropolitan Transit District (MTD):** MTD provides comprehensive bus services in Santa Barbara and the surrounding areas, including Goleta, Carpinteria, and Montecito. Buses are equipped with bike racks, making it convenient for cyclists.
- **Amtrak Train Service:** The Amtrak Pacific Surfliner connects Santa Barbara with other major California cities, offering a scenic and relaxing travel option. The train station is centrally located, close to the waterfront and downtown.
- **Shuttles and Taxis:** For direct travel, various shuttle services and taxi companies operate in the area, including rideshare options like Uber and Lyft, providing convenient transportation to and from the airport, hotels,

and key attractions.

By Bike

- **Bike-Friendly Community:** Santa Barbara is known for its bike-friendly atmosphere, with extensive bike lanes, trails, and dedicated paths, such as the Cabrillo Bike Path along the waterfront.
- **Bike Rentals and Tours:** Many shops in Santa Barbara offer bike rentals, including standard bicycles, electric bikes, and mountain bikes, allowing visitors to explore the area at their own pace. Guided bike tours are also available, offering a fun and informative way to see the city and its surroundings.
- **Cycling Events:** The community often hosts cycling events and group rides, which can be a great way to meet locals and experience the county's vibrant cycling culture.

Navigating Santa Barbara County can be a seamless and enjoyable experience, whether you're meandering through the lush vineyards of the Santa Ynez Valley by car, hopping on a bus to explore the historic sites, or cycling along the picturesque coastline. Each mode of transportation offers a unique perspective on the region's diverse landscapes and attractions, enhancing your visit to this beautiful part of California.

8

Itineraries

Itinerary 1: The Weekend Getaway – A 2-Day Trip Focusing on the Highlights

Embark on a weekend adventure in Santa Barbara to explore the city's quintessential attractions, from historic landmarks to stunning natural beauty. This 2-day itinerary is designed to offer a taste of what makes Santa Barbara a beloved destination.

Day 1: Discovering Downtown and the Waterfront

- **Morning: Explore State Street and Downtown**
- Start your day with breakfast at a local café on State Street, the vibrant artery of Santa Barbara, known for its Mediterranean-style architecture and palm-lined pathways.
- Stroll through downtown, visiting shops, galleries, and landmarks like the Santa Barbara County Courthouse, renowned for its Spanish Colonial Revival architecture and panoramic views from the clock tower.
- **Afternoon: Waterfront and Wharf**
- Head to the Santa Barbara Waterfront and walk along Cabrillo Boulevard to soak in the coastal beauty and visit the Stearns Wharf, where you can enjoy seafood, wine tasting, and ocean views.

- Visit the Santa Barbara Maritime Museum to learn about the region's rich nautical history, or take a relaxing cruise around the harbor.
- **Evening: Dinner and Sunset**
- Dine at one of the waterfront restaurants, indulging in fresh local seafood or Californian cuisine while watching the sunset.
- Conclude your evening with a leisurely walk along the beach or enjoy a live performance at one of Santa Barbara's theaters.

Day 2: Nature and Wine Country

- **Morning: Natural Beauty**
- Begin your day with a hike in the Santa Barbara foothills, choosing trails like Inspiration Point for stunning city and ocean views, or explore the Santa Barbara Botanic Garden to appreciate native California plants.
- **Afternoon: Santa Ynez Valley Wine Tasting**
- Venture into the Santa Ynez Valley, a short drive from Santa Barbara, and spend your afternoon wine tasting at local vineyards. The valley is known for its excellent Pinot Noir, Chardonnay, and Syrah.
- Enjoy lunch at a winery or one of the charming restaurants in towns like Los Olivos or Solvang, a Danish-themed village with unique shops and bakeries.
- **Evening: Return to Santa Barbara**
- Head back to Santa Barbara for a casual dinner in the Funk Zone, the city's artsy and eclectic district, where you can enjoy local art, craft breweries, and urban wine tasting rooms.
- Wrap up your weekend with a stroll along the Funk Zone's murals or catch live music at a local venue.

This 2-day itinerary in Santa Barbara offers a balanced mix of urban exploration, natural beauty, and the culinary delights of wine country, making for a perfect weekend getaway that captures the essence of this picturesque Californian city.

ITINERARIES

Itinerary 2: Family Vacation – A 5-Day Plan with Family-Friendly Activities

Embark on a memorable 5-day family vacation in Santa Barbara, where the city's laid-back charm, beautiful landscapes, and kid-friendly attractions come together to create the perfect getaway for all ages.

Day 1: Downtown Discovery and Beach Fun

- **Morning: Downtown Exploration**
- Start your family adventure with a visit to the Santa Barbara Museum of Natural History, where interactive exhibits delight kids and adults alike.
- Stroll down State Street, enjoying the shops and outdoor dining. Don't miss the Santa Barbara Public Market for a variety of food options.
- **Afternoon: Beach Time**
- Spend the afternoon at East Beach, where the soft sands and gentle waves make for a family-friendly beach experience. Enjoy beach volleyball, playgrounds, and the waterfront bike path.
- **Evening: Casual Dinner on the Wharf**
- Dine at Stearns Wharf, where seafood restaurants offer dishes for every palate, and the views at sunset are spectacular. Visit the candy store or ice cream shops for a sweet treat.

Day 2: Mission and Museum Day

- **Morning: Historical Exploration**
- Visit the iconic Santa Barbara Mission to learn about local history and enjoy the beautiful rose garden. The mission offers self-guided tours suitable for children.
- **Afternoon: Hands-On Learning**
- Head to MOXI, The Wolf Museum of Exploration + Innovation, where interactive science exhibits engage curious minds. Children can experiment, play, and learn about various scientific principles.
- **Evening: Relaxing Dinner**

- Enjoy a family dinner at a kid-friendly restaurant in the downtown area, with many options featuring menus that cater to younger guests.

Day 3: Zoo Adventure and Waterfront Activities

- **Morning: Zoo Exploration**
- Spend the morning at the Santa Barbara Zoo, a compact but diverse zoo perfect for young children. Don't miss the chance to feed the giraffes!
- **Afternoon: Harbor and Sea Life**
- Explore the Santa Barbara Harbor, where you can take a boat tour or visit the Sea Center to touch sea creatures and learn about marine life.
- **Evening: Sunset and Stroll**
- Have a casual dinner at the harbor and end the day with a sunset walk along the breakwater, watching the boats and enjoying the ocean breeze.

Day 4: Outdoor Adventures and Scenic Drives

- **Morning: Nature Walk or Botanic Garden**
- Go for a family hike in Santa Barbara's nature preserves or visit the Santa Barbara Botanic Garden to explore native plants and scenic trails.
- **Afternoon: Scenic Drive and Picnic**
- Drive up to the Santa Ynez Mountains for breathtaking views. Pack a picnic and enjoy the natural beauty of places like Knapp's Castle or Lizard's Mouth.
- **Evening: Dinner in Town**
- Return to Santa Barbara for dinner, perhaps trying one of the many family-friendly eateries with a relaxed atmosphere and diverse menus.

Day 5: Leisure Day and Departure

- **Morning: Leisure Activities**
- Use your last day for leisure activities based on family interests. You could revisit a favorite spot, explore a local park, or do some last-minute

shopping in unique boutiques.
- **Afternoon: Farewell to Santa Barbara**
- Enjoy a farewell lunch or early dinner before heading home, reflecting on the memories made and the fun experiences shared in Santa Barbara.

This 5-day family vacation itinerary in Santa Barbara offers educational experiences, outdoor adventures, and relaxing beach days, ensuring that every family member has an enjoyable and memorable stay.

Itinerary 3: The Outdoor Enthusiast – A Week-Long Adventure Exploring Nature

For those who crave the outdoors and seek adventure in natural settings, Santa Barbara provides a stunning backdrop for a week-long exploration of diverse landscapes, from coastal beaches to rugged mountains. Here's a detailed itinerary for outdoor enthusiasts looking to immerse themselves in the natural beauty of Santa Barbara County.

Day 1: Coastal Exploration and Beach Activities

- **Morning: Hiking and Views**
- Begin with a hike up the Mesa Trail to enjoy panoramic views of the coastline and the Channel Islands.
- **Afternoon: Beach Time**
- Spend the afternoon at Arroyo Burro Beach, also known as Hendry's Beach, perfect for surfing, beachcombing, or simply relaxing by the ocean.
- **Evening: Seafood Dinner**
- Enjoy a fresh seafood dinner at a waterfront restaurant, savoring the local catch while watching the sunset.

Day 2: Mountain Adventures and Scenic Views

- **Morning: Mountain Hiking**

- Tackle the challenging but rewarding hike up to Inspiration Point or Cathedral Peak, offering breathtaking views of the city and beyond.
- **Afternoon: Botanical Exploration**
- Visit the Santa Barbara Botanic Garden to wind down and explore the native plant life and serene walking trails.
- **Evening: Relaxing Night**
- Return to town for a casual dinner, perhaps trying one of Santa Barbara's farm-to-table restaurants.

Day 3: Water Sports and Harbor Life

- **Morning: Kayaking or Stand-Up Paddleboarding**
- Head to the Santa Barbara Harbor to rent kayaks or paddleboards, exploring the coastline and possibly spotting marine life.
- **Afternoon: Maritime Museum**
- Visit the Santa Barbara Maritime Museum to learn about the region's nautical history and ocean conservation.
- **Evening: Harbor Dining**
- Dine at a harborside restaurant, enjoying the fresh ocean breeze and local cuisine.

Day 4: Channel Islands Adventure

- **Full Day: Channel Islands National Park**
- Take a boat trip to the Channel Islands National Park for a day of hiking, wildlife watching, and unparalleled natural beauty. The islands offer a remote wilderness experience with unique flora and fauna.

Day 5: Cycling and Urban Nature

- **Morning: Bike Ride**
- Rent a bicycle and ride along the Cabrillo Bike Path, enjoying coastal views and stopping at beaches or parks along the way.

- **Afternoon: Urban Nature Walk**
- Explore the urban nature trails, such as the Alice Keck Park Memorial Gardens or the Douglas Family Preserve, for a blend of city and nature.
- **Evening: Downtown Santa Barbara**
- Enjoy the evening in downtown Santa Barbara, with options for dining, shopping, and entertainment.

Day 6: Backcountry Exploration

- **Full Day: Los Padres National Forest**
- Venture into the Los Padres National Forest for a day of hiking or mountain biking in the backcountry, exploring the diverse ecosystems and rugged terrain.

Day 7: Leisure and Departure

- **Morning: Leisure Time**
- Spend your last morning enjoying a leisurely activity, like a beach walk, bird watching at the Andree Clark Bird Refuge, or visiting a local farmers' market.
- **Afternoon: Departure**
- Reflect on a week of adventure and natural beauty as you prepare to depart, taking with you memories of an exhilarating outdoor experience in Santa Barbara.

This itinerary for the outdoor enthusiast offers a comprehensive exploration of Santa Barbara's natural wonders, from coastal pleasures to mountainous escapades and the unique environment of the Channel Islands, ensuring a week filled with adventure and discovery.

9

Local Tips and Tricks

Insider Knowledge: How to Avoid the Crowds and Make the Most of Your Visit

Exploring Santa Barbara like a local means knowing how to sidestep the tourist throngs and uncovering the hidden gems of this picturesque coastal city. Here are insider tips to help you avoid the crowds and maximize your experience in Santa Barbara.

Visit During Off-Peak Times

- **Seasonal Considerations:** While summer and holiday weekends are peak tourist seasons, visiting in the shoulder months like late spring (April to early June) or early fall (September to October) can offer milder weather and fewer crowds.
- **Time of Day:** Early mornings or late afternoons are ideal for visiting popular spots like the Santa Barbara Mission or the beaches, as you'll avoid the midday rush and can enjoy a more serene experience.

Explore Lesser-Known Attractions

- **Hidden Beaches:** Instead of the busy East Beach or Butterfly Beach, try

the more secluded Loon Point or Haskell's Beach for a quiet day by the ocean.
- **Quiet Hiking Trails:** While Inspiration Point and Rattlesnake Canyon are popular, consider hiking in the less frequented areas of the Santa Ynez Mountains, such as San Ysidro Trail or the Cold Spring Trail.

Dine Like a Local

- **Off-the-Beaten-Path Restaurants:** Skip the tourist-heavy eateries along State Street and opt for local favorites in the Mesa, Goleta, or the Santa Ynez Valley, where you can find excellent food without the wait.
- **Non-Peak Dining Hours:** Enjoy meals during non-peak hours; a late lunch or an early dinner can mean better service and a more relaxed atmosphere.

Stay in Alternative Accommodations

- **Outside the City Center:** Consider staying in accommodations just outside the main city center, such as in Carpinteria or Goleta, where you can enjoy a quieter setting and often better rates.
- **Vacation Rentals and B&Bs:** Opt for a vacation rental, boutique inn, or bed and breakfast in residential neighborhoods for a more authentic and less crowded experience.

Utilize Local Transportation

- **Biking and Walking:** Santa Barbara is extremely bike-friendly, with numerous trails and lanes throughout the city. Walking or biking can be a more intimate way to see the area and avoid parking hassles.
- **Public Transit:** Take advantage of the local bus system or the waterfront shuttle for convenient and inexpensive travel around town, bypassing the need to find parking in busy areas.

LOCAL TIPS AND TRICKS

Engage in Local Culture and Events

- **Community Events:** Check out local newspapers or websites for community events, farmers' markets, and neighborhood festivals, which offer a taste of local life and culture away from tourist-centric activities.
- **Shop Local:** Visit local shops and boutiques off the main tourist strips for unique finds and a more leisurely shopping experience.

By integrating these insider tips into your travel plans, you can experience the charm and beauty of Santa Barbara without the crowds, making your visit truly memorable and enjoyable.

10

Conclusion

Parting Words: Encouragement to Explore and Create Your Own Santa Barbara Story

As you prepare to embark on your journey to Santa Barbara, remember that this enchanting city is more than just a destination; it's a backdrop for creating your own unique story. With its stunning landscapes, rich cultural tapestry, and welcoming community, Santa Barbara offers endless possibilities for exploration, discovery, and personal connection.

Embrace the Adventure

- Venture beyond the well-trodden paths to uncover hidden gems and local favorites. Whether it's a secluded beach, a quaint café, or a scenic hiking trail, Santa Barbara is full of surprises waiting to be discovered.

Connect with the Community

- Engage with the locals and immerse yourself in the city's vibrant culture. Attend community events, visit local markets, and participate in festivals to experience the true spirit of Santa Barbara.

CONCLUSION

Savor Every Moment

- Take the time to appreciate the natural beauty and relaxed pace of life in Santa Barbara. Watch the sunset from the waterfront, enjoy a leisurely stroll through the historic streets, and savor the flavors of the local cuisine.

Create Lasting Memories

- Your trip to Santa Barbara is an opportunity to create lasting memories, whether you're traveling solo, with a partner, or with family. Capture moments through photos, journaling, or simply by being present in the experience.

Leave with Gratitude

- As your visit comes to a close, reflect on the experiences and connections you've made. Leave with a sense of gratitude for the memories and the people who have made your Santa Barbara story unique and meaningful.

Santa Barbara, with its blend of natural beauty, cultural richness, and friendly ambiance, is more than just a place to visit; it's a place to live, learn, and create stories that last a lifetime. So go forth with an open heart and curious spirit, ready to weave your own narrative into the tapestry of this extraordinary city. Your Santa Barbara story awaits.

Resources: Further Reading and Useful Websites for Planning Your Trip to Santa Barbara

To make the most of your Santa Barbara adventure, it's essential to have access to reliable and comprehensive resources. Below are some recommended readings and websites that will help you plan your trip, discover hidden gems, and learn more about what this beautiful city has to offer.

Official Tourism Websites

- **Visit Santa Barbara:** SantaBarbaraCA.com
- The official tourism website for Santa Barbara, offering a wealth of information on accommodations, dining, activities, and events.
- **Santa Barbara County's Official Website:** SantaBarbaraCounty.gov
- Provides insights into the region's services, parks, and historical sites, along with practical information for visitors.

Travel Guides and Blogs

- **Lonely Planet - Santa Barbara:**
- Offers comprehensive travel guides and tips, highlighting top attractions, local eateries, and activities.
- **Travel + Leisure - Santa Barbara Guide:**
- Features articles, recommendations, and reviews on Santa Barbara's luxury and budget travel options, including personal travel blogs and stories.

Local News and Event Calendars

- **Santa Barbara Independent:** Independent.com
- A local newspaper that covers current events, cultural happenings, and community news, including a calendar of local events and festivals.
- **Noozhawk:** Noozhawk.com
- Provides local news, including sections on lifestyle and entertainment,

CONCLUSION

which are great for catching up on upcoming events and local happenings.

Outdoor and Recreational Resources

- **Santa Barbara Hikes:** SantaBarbaraHikes.com
- A resource for finding the best hikes in and around Santa Barbara, complete with trail guides and difficulty ratings.
- **Channel Islands National Park:** NPS.gov/chis
- The official National Park Service site for the Channel Islands, offering planning tips for visits, including boat schedules, hiking trails, and conservation efforts.

Cultural and Historical Insights

- **Santa Barbara Historical Museum:** SBHistorical.org
- Explore Santa Barbara's rich history through the museum's online resources and exhibit information.
- **Santa Barbara Mission:** SBMission.org
- Provides historical background, visiting hours, and event information for one of Santa Barbara's most iconic landmarks.

Transportation Information

- **Santa Barbara Metropolitan Transit District (MTD):** SBMTD.gov
- The main public transportation provider in Santa Barbara, offering bus routes, schedules, and fare information.

These resources offer a solid foundation for planning your Santa Barbara trip, whether you're looking for relaxation, adventure, cultural immersion, or all of the above. With the right information at your fingertips, you're well-equipped to create an itinerary that suits your interests and to craft a memorable experience in the enchanting city of Santa Barbara.

11

Appendices

Accommodations Contact Information:

Luxury Resorts

1. **Four Seasons Resort The Biltmore Santa Barbara**: 805-969-2261; fourseasons.com
2. **The Ritz-Carlton Bacara, Santa Barbara**: 805-968-0100; ritzcarlton.com
3. **Belmond El Encanto**: 805-845-5800; belmond.com

Boutique Hotels

1. **Hotel Californian**: 805-882-0100; hotelcalifornian.com
2. **Kimpton Canary Hotel**: 805-884-0300; canarysantabarbara.com

Mid-Range Hotels

1. **The Wayfarer**: 805-335-2033; marriott.com
2. **Harbor House Inn**: 805-962-9748; harborhouseinn.com

3. **Hotel Milo Santa Barbara**: 805-965-4577; hotelmilosantabarbara.com

Budget-Friendly Options

1. **Agave Inn**: 805-687-6009; agaveinnsb.com
2. **The Presidio**: 805-963-1355; presidiosb.com

Bed and Breakfasts

1. **Simpson House Inn**: 805-963-7067; simpsonhouseinn.com
2. **Cheshire Cat Inn**: 805-569-1610; cheshirecat.com
3. **The Eagle Inn**: 805-965-3586; theeagleinn.com

Vacation Rentals and Unique Stays

1. **Santa Barbara Beachfront Rentals**: 805-275-1851; paradiseretreats.com
2. **AutoCamp Santa Barbara**: 888-405-7553; autocamp.com

Adventures

1. Captain Jack's Tours: 805-608-5765; captainjackstours.com
2. Condor Express Whale Watching: 805-882-0088; condorexpress.com
3. santabarbarara.com
4. santabarbarahikes.com
5. Land Shark Tours: 805-683-7600; landsharktours.com
6. Santa Barbara Wine Tours: 805-965-1414; winetours-santabarbara.com
7. Wine Country Tours: 805-364-5979; 805winecountrytours.com
8. Appellation Wine Tours: 707-299-9463: appellationwinetours.com
9. Stagecoach Co. Wine Tours Inc.: winetourssantaynez.com

APPENDICES

10. Sustainable Wine Tours: 805-698-3911; sustainablewinetours.com

Links to Maps of Santa Barbara

https://images.app.goo.gl/HNJMRZT8Y8pJu9Pm9

https://images.app.goo.gl/QJDRkJm6NBT7XZSe6

https://www.mapz.com/maps/Santa_Barbara

https://californiawineryadvisor.com/santa-barbara-wine-maps/